Praise for *Alive with Spirits*

"Truly a gift to witches everywhere, Althaea Sebastiani's *Alive with Spirits* is grounded firmly in lived experience. A wonderful and moving introduction to animism, as well as a fantastic introduction to witchcraft; even the seasoned practitioner will gain so much from reading Sebastiani's offering. Moving us away from a witchcraft rooted in materialism, individualism, and objectification, *Alive with Spirits* provides the tools and knowledge to pave a path that is instead rooted in true community with the Land. The many exercises and knowledge provided within these pages ask us to move away from ideas of ascension or move beyond our bodies to instead relish in the magic that can only be found in being entirely human and at one with our physicality. A book I will truly recommend to many for years to come! I am deeply thankful this book exists."

—Mhara Starling, author of *Welsh Witchcraft*

"Whether you're just starting your journey or you've been on the path of the witch for many years, this book will change you. By taking us through the five traits of witchcraft and the seven skills that create a foundation for practicing witchcraft effectively, Althaea Sebastiani gives to us first a broad overview of what a witch can learn that will enhance their practice before delving into lessons and exercises that lead to a stronger sense of self in who we are as witches. While I was reading, I realized I will be spending quite a bit of time on some of the lessons due to the journal work and the exercises, which I can foresee becoming part of my practice. This is most definitely not a book to rush through. I know that it will change my worldview, a process that is never comfortable; but with a calm and gentle hand, Althaea takes us, step by step, through the lessons, which makes it easy to open our trust to her."

—Christine Cunningham Ashworth, author of *Scott Cunningham—The Path Taken*

"A talented, accessible teacher and experienced witch, Althaea Sebastiani offers insight into what's missing from modern witchcraft, which has become so commercialized. Tying together the animist worldview with practices geared toward being in right relationship with spirits and the land, she addresses the philosophical, sociopolitical, and practical currents of witchcraft in a deeply satisfying way. As a worldview rather than a belief system, animism has many culturally specific iterations all over the globe, and Althaea's focus on local land and community connections prevents the umbrella of animism from becoming falsely universalizing. Reflecting what is so effective about the classes she teaches, Althaea's writing is straightforward, practical, and actionable, organized into discrete lessons with hands-on exercises. Regardless of one's specific beliefs about god(s) and/or goddess(es), *Alive with Spirits* is clarifying, grounding, and a breath of fresh air for magic practitioners at every level."

—Lane Smith, author of *Seventy-Eight Acts of Liberation: Tarot to Transform our World*

"Althaea Sebastiani has written a robust but incredibly accessible guide to becoming a relational witch, informed by decades of direct experience with the Land as teacher. The guidance in *Alive with Spirits* will awaken your awareness of the web of relationships around you, breathe life into your magickal works, and help you build a life and practice oriented around community—with human and more-than-human spirits alike."

—Sarah Corbett, founder and lead herbalist of Rowan + Sage

Alive with Spirits

The Path
and Practice
of Animistic
Witchcraft

Althaea Sebastiani

WEISER BOOKS

This edition first published in 2024 by Weiser Books, an imprint of
Red Wheel/Weiser, LLC
With offices at:
65 Parker Street, Suite 7
Newburyport, MA 01950
www.redwheelweiser.com

Library of Congress Cataloging-in-Publication Data

Names: Sebastiani, Althaea, author.
Title: Alive with spirits : the path and practice of animistic witchcraft / Althaea Sebastiani.
Other titles: Path and practice of animistic witchcraft
Description: Newburyport, MA : Weiser Books, 2024. | Summary: "At the root of most
    spiritual traditions is the aspiration to realize one's birthright: the intimate connection
    with the land and the spiritual energies that inhabit it. This connection with the
    land and its spirits is a worldview known as animism. This book explores animism
    in a hands-on way that teaches through firsthand, direct experiences and embodied
    exercises based in wholeness, providing a firm foundation from which to transform
    your witchcraft practice"—Provided by publisher.
Identifiers: LCCN 2024000053 | ISBN 9781578638253 (trade paperback) |
    ISBN 9781633413245 (ebook)
Subjects: LCSH: Witchcraft. | Animism. | BISAC: BODY, MIND & SPIRIT /
    Witchcraft (see also RELIGION / Wicca) | BODY, MIND & SPIRIT /
    Magick Studies
Classification: LCC BF1566 .S395 2024 | DDC 133.4/3—dc23/eng/20240226
LC record available at https://lccn.loc.gov/2024000053

Cover design by Sky Peck Design
Cover image by iStock/Vizerskaya
Interior by Debby Dutton
Typeset in Adobe Jenson, Aller, and Astralaga

Printed in the United States of America
IBI
10 9 8 7 6 5 4 3 2 1

For the yucca and the oak,
for the mountains and the marshes,
for the voices that reach across continents
and whisper of family and home.

Contents

Exercise List

Lesson 1 Witchcraft and Worldview
Exercise 1: Identifying Worldview—Journal Prompt
Assessing the ways witchcraft impacts your thoughts, perceptions, and interactions.
Exercise 2: Scavenger Hunt—Energy Exercise
Becoming familiar with how energy feels by comparing the energy of various objects before and after centering.

Lesson 2 Witchcraft Comes from the Land
Exercise 1: Identifying Obstacles and Opportunities—Journal Prompt
Assessing the ways animism is already present in your life and the ways through which it could be more present.
Exercise 2: Push and Pull—Energy Exercise
Practicing feeling and moving energy by forming energy balls.
Exercise 3: Becoming a Local Witch
Gaining familiarity with your local land through gaining familiarity with local plants.

Ongoing Exercises

Lesson 3 A World Alive with Spirits
Exercise 1: Practicing Discernment—Energy Exercise
Learning to recognize differences in energy.
Exercise 2: Grounding—Energy Exercise
Grounding via creating an energetic circuit within the body.
Exercises 3: To Be Aware
Practicing awareness skills through visiting a nearby location outside.
Ongoing Exercises

Lesson 4 Being in Community
Exercise 1: Contemplating Community—Journal Prompt
Examining thoughts and experiences with community.
Exercise 2: Discerning Your Edges—Energy Exercise
Strengthening awareness of spiritual boundaries.
Exercises 3: Being a Good Housemate
Increasing awareness of house spirits by introducing yourself to them.
Ongoing Exercises

Lesson 5 The Layered Witch
Exercise 1: Defining Your Borders—Energy Exercise
Moving energy through your spirit body and along its edges.
Exercise 2: Entering Trance
Comparing different methods for entering trance.
Exercise 3: Progress Check—Journal Prompt
Assessing experiences with the exercises so far.
Ongoing Exercises

Introduction

What is life as a witch but an unfolding conversation, but an experience of becoming more and more entangled with the Land? In many ways, the practice of witchcraft exists as an interplay between ourselves and the Land—a term to denote the intersection of the physical world and the very real spirits that call the land home. Witchcraft exists within that connection, enlivened by it, and made something that is capable of reaching out and taking hold of us as strongly as we reach out and dare try to wrap our hands about it.

A land-based approach to witchcraft is necessarily grounded in relationship with the Land, yet not in a way that is founded on archetypes and objectification but in awareness and acknowledgment that our world is so very much larger than we may have been led to believe, that it is filled with a greater variety of people than we may have yet encountered. This awareness is encompassed by the worldview known as animism. Within the context of contemporary witchcraft, animism is the definitive influence behind a land-based approach. It provides structure for practice that is rooted in deep relationship with physicality, both of the land and of ourselves. It affords us a sense of connection to something larger than ourselves that is gained through an understanding of community that includes individual spirits as much as it includes other humans.

For this reason, animist witchcraft demands an intimacy with life itself, urging us to confront the many influences we carry that keep us holding back and living in such a way as to maintain separation between ourselves and the land, between ourselves and each other. And yet many obstacles exist to us.

Animism is the oldest known worldview among humankind, flourishing throughout the world and throughout history. Although it is still quite prevalent, the obstacles many of us face in embodying animism are actively maintained by Euro-American society—a term that encompasses what might also be termed "Western society" and thus includes those countries shaped and defined by colonial thinking. These countries tend to also be structured around systems that actively work to discourage the community-based understanding of the world espoused by animism and instead encourage us to believe we are separate from each other, separate from the land, and that our survival is dependent upon competition rather than community, connection, and obligation to each other.

As such, the dominant worldview of Euro-American society has frequently destroyed animist societies from the inside out, resulting in consequences that we all live through in different ways. For some of us, that means unlearning to think of our experiences and perspective as universal and the default for all people. For others, it means discovering that there is a potential way of being in the world that matches what we knew to be true but couldn't find the words to describe. And for others still, it means finding new ways to hold on to the beauty of what persisted within our own families and cultures despite the efforts of these systems of power.

In many ways, this book is a handbook for inscendence—for sinking oneself deeper into the land, into physicality, into the wonder that is life and living—and for building deep relationships with the many spirits with whom we share this world. It is a means of support while working to actively peel back the layers of overculture (meaning the dominant culture in a society) influence that keep us searching for connection yet unable to find and hold on to it. It is a source of guidance to discover the layering of spirit world and physical world, how that same layering is present within us, and how embracing the existence of that layering can help us to discover wholeness within the land and ourselves. It is a reminder of a worldview that exists as the birthright of humanity, that is available to us to reclaim, and that holds true potential for us to forge intimate relationships with the land and its spirits.

As demonstration of that potential, much of the guidance contained in this book is directly born of spirit whisper. It is grounded in lived experience: in conversations with oak trees that hold the meadow clear and shady with the expanse of their branches, in realizations had while watching trolls fish on the other side of a mountain stream, in moonlit walks surrounded by laughing coyotes, in the smiles of family members—lined with age— recognizing when reminders of proper etiquette with farm spirits were no longer needed. There are energy exercises in these pages literally taught to me by spirits who linger in the shadows of trees, their whispers filtered through an awareness of self and a collection of experiences that allow for the skills necessary for similar conversations and experiences to be taught to others. Likewise, the concept of community and its importance—a value stressed throughout this book—comes from my experience of being raised in a collectivist culture. In this culture, community wasn't something that we worked toward but something woven so deeply into life that it wouldn't be until I was a young adult that I would realize that not everyone's families operated that way.

So, while this book is, in so many ways, a guide to help you discover your own potential for a witchcraft defined by relationship with the Land, it is also a compilation of my personal experiences, of insight and expertise gleaned through learning witchcraft directly from spirits, through a lifetime spent in rural and remote places, through being part of a minoritized ethnic group and navigating the incompatibilities between family culture and overculture. These are influences that I carry with me and that define how I approach, teach, and write about witchcraft and animism. And while that means there are times when this approach will irreconcilably crash head first into forms of witchcraft with which many of us are familiar, I can say with full confidence that means of navigating the incompatibility not only exist, but are also achievable.

This is why there's been an attempt to be radically inclusive. There is a lot of consideration throughout the book: the exercise list, the repetition, defining of terms, section recaps, final notes, glossary, disclaimers in exercises, noting how long exercises take, exercise outlines . . . these are all accommodations for the neurodivergent, the disabled, and other marginalized populations.

With hope, this book will help you to uncover what that navigation might look like for you.

Lesson 1

Witchcraft and Worldview

In every moment, you exist as one being in a world thrumming and alive with spirits. Though you may sit alone, reading these words, the potential for connection that exists to you, right now, with innumerable beings that you encounter every day—who are near to you even in this moment—is striking. There is no tool nor special power needed for you to establish that connection and to begin building relationships with any of these spirit beings. Rather, the ability to be aware of the presence of these spirits is open to everyone. It is intrinsic to what it means to be human, as natural as our need to reach for each other, to build relationships, and form community.

Animism is the oldest known worldview—a way of seeing the world that extends belonging and community to the non-human people with whom we share the Earth. Throughout the course of this book, we will work together to peel back the layers that occlude our awareness of these spirit beings—an occlusion impressed upon us by a society focused on individualism to such an extent that it leaves us feeling separated and alone. You'll discover firsthand that connection to something more—to the Otherworld and to the spirits with whom you share your home and share the land—is very possible. By focusing on what it means to be in right relationship with others, this book will help you to further seat yourself in the web of connection, affording you a greater sense of support from and wholeness within the world.

But before we get too deep . . .

As a worldview, animism belongs to no single religion, ethnic group, or culture. It is the oldest known worldview among humans and can be found throughout the world. As a term, animism was coined by Sir Edward Burnett Tylor in *Primitive Culture*, which has all the problems one would expect of a work published in 1871, (such as racist views toward Indigenous people and a repugnant attitude toward non-Christian religion). His work was highly influential and helped solidify the standard of viewing Indigenous and non-Christian religions as scholarly curiosities, to be studied, extracted, and presented by elite white people for acclaim. This attitude continues to not only be widespread but also the default in academia and is thus replicated in circles where one would expect otherwise, such as various non-Christian spiritual communities. As witches seeking to reclaim our connection with the land and its spirits, we can do better.

In presenting a form of animism that is firmly rooted within contemporary witchcraft, it is important to distinguish that this animism does not come from nor is influenced by any Indigenous culture. Rather, the animism found within this book is based on my personal experience as a spirit-led witch, experience that stretches across nearly three decades and is predominantly influenced by

Alive with Spirits

direct interactions with a wide range of spirits—many of whose words, teachings, and techniques have directly contributed to the material you now read.

As such, the animism herein can and will differ from other animisms, as the filtering of this worldview through a cultural context absolutely alters significant details, such as the nature of and qualifications for personhood. As we'll delve into in Lesson 3: A World Alive with Spirits, we will be approaching personhood in an expansive way, erasing the degree of separation among humans, spirits, and the unknown in a way that those spirits who helped shape this material would find most pleasing. With this expansive definition of personhood, we also help combat the academic view of animism, a view that keeps it impersonal and, largely, a thought experiment rather than lived.

What Is Witchcraft?

Witchcraft, as it is commonly known and practiced, is a contemporary magickal system rooted in European folk magic practices. The ambiguity of the word European is, unfortunately, accurate in this context as modern witchcraft (with incredibly few exceptions) does not exist as a continuation of practice of any specific people's folk magic. Rather it is largely reimagined and innovated; something altogether new. It is a method of inspiriting the folkloric essence into the context of contemporary Western culture in a way that helps us to feel more connected to the physical world and to each other.

Because of this, witchcraft is a spiritual practice with a clearly determinable history that stretches backward only several decades and, as such, is easily traced and has been extensively documented. While tracing that history, however briefly, is outside the scope of this book, it is enough for us to emphasize that (a) witchcraft is not ancient, (b) witchcraft is not the continued practice of any Indigenous European people, and (c) because it is wholly modern, witchcraft is open to everyone, regardless of cultural background. If you feel the call to witchcraft, you belong here and no one can tell you otherwise.

In holding to a definition of witchcraft that refers specifically to a contemporary practice with a documented history, the distinction between it and two commonly conflated terms warrants examination—these terms are folk magic and witchcraft in the historical accusatory usage.

Folk magic is a body of information relative to the common people of a specific region that relates to spiritual beliefs, superstitions, customs, and the position that people hold within the local land, as well as those practices utilized to better help the individual and their community navigate that position, be in right relationship with the land and its spirits, and otherwise better their position in life. What truly defines folk magic is its *folk*—the specific ethnic group that holds those beliefs and practices and who maintain those beliefs and practices as part of their living culture. One can read about a culture in which they were not raised, but that doesn't make them a part of that community. It doesn't make them part of the folk.

And so, despite taking inspiration from the folk magic of various European ethnic groups (sometimes quite liberally), this doesn't make those folk magic practices witchcraft. This is especially true when you consider that many of these folk magic practices have existed in some form for far longer than contemporary witchcraft, these practices originated and operate within a thoroughly Christianized context (whereas contemporary witchcraft exists as part of the Pagan religious movement), and the people of these ethnic groups would likely be appalled to be referred to as witches (especially true the further back you go in time or if any of these ethnic groups were historically accused of being "witches" as part of ongoing stigma against them).

Attempted imitation based in inspiration—regardless of how respectfully conducted—does not mean that one belongs to the community from which that practice originates. Likewise, it also does not mean an unbroken line of practice in regard to folkloric practices from a specific point in time. The attempt to revive folk magic practices no longer practiced within its originating ethnic group (based on historical accounts) within a contemporary witchcraft context does not make those practices witchcraft and it does not mean that we can trace a continuous line of witchcraft going back a few hundred years—not without great intellectual dishonesty.

This absolutely includes those bits and pieces that have been gleaned from historical accounts of the witch trials. Contemporary witchcraft has no direct connection to historical accusatory witchcraft. The contexts surrounding the use of the words witch and witchcraft are so different between the two that they may as well be using different words altogether.

This quickly becomes obvious in considering the sociopolitical (and religious) climate of the time and that no one who was tried as a witch would have ever referred to themselves as such—the term referred more so to a supernatural being than a living human. Accusations were frequently the result of interpersonal drama and scapegoating, not because the accused was doing anything that would resemble our own concepts of magick and witchcraft. That there were folk magic practitioners—who had their own names for their craft—who existed in these time periods and who had practices we find inspiring and imagine to be similar to our own practices does not mean that these practitioners were witches or that we should be foisting such a label onto them.

As a practice, witchcraft demands an intimacy with our lives. It requires us to know who we are, where we live, and who lives there with us. This is part of the defining flavor of this practice: witchcraft prizes the physical—whether that be the physical world, our physical bodies, or the physical tools and objects so prevalent within this craft. There are other aspects that define this craft, too, in addition to its irrevocable embracing of the physical. In differentiating witchcraft from the numerous other magickal systems that exist, we can point to five distinct traits. These traits are:

- animism

- divination

- the Land

- ritual

- spirit work

Animism

This is the foundational worldview of contemporary witchcraft; the essence that infuses all other traits, the context that determines how action is taken. At the most fundamental level, animism is the belief that everything holds a spirit with whom you can communicate and interact. But, as you'll explore throughout this book, that definition doesn't begin to scratch the surface. There is a depth to animism that quickly becomes the water in which you swim, the air you breath, the beating of the heart inside your chest.

Although discussion of animism within the general magickal community has become more common in recent years, animism is the oldest and most pervasive worldview among humans. It can be found across the planet, throughout time, and among innumerable cultures. It is important to understand, however, that animism is not a religion. Nor is it something that can be practiced. Rather, animism is a worldview, an all-encompassing way of being that affects not just your spiritual practice, but also the way that you live your life.

It's also important to understand that animism is expressed differently within different cultural contexts. So, the animism that is found within and expressed through witchcraft differs from the animism expressed through various Indigenous cultures—and the animism expressed through those individual Indigenous cultures will very likely differ from each other, too. This does not mean that anyone is "doing animism wrong" but rather is an acknowledgment that worldviews are shared and that specific cultural contexts means the actions taken based upon a shared worldview will be different because different religions are different, and different cultures are different. These differences are a good thing. Diversity is the natural state of our world.

Divination

Of these five traits that together (and not individually) constitute witchcraft, perhaps the clearest example is divination. Divination is any variety of methods of gathering information, through the use of spiritual skills to analyze and interpret spiritual forces, that are reliant upon the use of physical objects. This means that successful (that is, accurate and precise) use of divination is dependent upon the cultivation and honing of skill in order to sense and interpret energy (spiritual forces) and/or sense and communicate with spiritual beings.

There is no single divination modality that is common among witches. Likewise, there is no single divination method that you must know and practice in order to be a witch (to put that another way, you can be a witch and never touch a Tarot deck). What all divination methods have in common is that they rely on random variables in order to, essentially, take a snapshot of the energy currents surrounding a person, situation, or both, as they presently exist or as they exist in the future, based upon the way things are at this present moment. The ways in which each divination modality achieves their results is how those methods differ, and also why each method has its own strengths and limitations. This is why it's good to be familiar with multiple divination systems.

We see animism present in divination in the way that divination so very often is a conversation between the witch and spirits, with various divination tools used as mediaries for conversation

with Gods, ancestors, and other spirits. We also see how some divination methods are dependent upon a strong relationship with
spirits, such as throwing the bones. This is distinct from methods
of divination that rely upon interpretation (whether intuitively or
logically) as the primary means of interpreting the information
attained via divining.

The Land

With purposeful capitalization, "the Land" refers to the intersection of the physical world with the spirits that inhabit it, particularly those spirits whom would be termed "land spirits." It is this
intersection from which witchcraft is born, rising up as a whisper
that calls and sings to those who would dare to see how much more
there is to the world than they've been told. It is the conjoined forces
of physicality and spirituality, the unique expression of being that is
possible only within the container of physicality and with the vast
potential of being that exists without it. It is the form that holds the
liminal, the doorway through which we step and that upon which
we walk as we pass through it. It is the wholeness that consumes
once we dissolve the idea of separation that exists between the
physical world and the spirit world—between our physical bodies
and our spirit bodies; it is the connection that binds all to all.

When we speak of land spirits, it is individual beings—people,
like you and me—to whom we are referring. It is the whispers of
these people that guide and shape this craft. It is from them that
we can learn the entirety of witchcraft, whether that be methods
for protecting ourselves, what herbs to use to purify our homes, or
even techniques for calling and communicating with the dead. And

it is in them that we can discover powerful allies, trusted companions, and warm friends. There is no witchcraft without the Land. It is the force behind our magick—the objects and tools we use within our spells. It is our anchor, our sustainer, the very source of witchcraft.

Ritual

In defining magick as the action of utilizing spiritual forces to create change, ritual is any series of steps that can be repeated in order to consistently achieve similar results. When you carefully harvest herbs in the early morning, stripping leaf from stem before drying them in a cool dark place with good airflow, and then tuck them away in a tight sealing jar and hide them from the sun's kiss, you are performing a ritual for the sake of obtaining high quality herb matter.

When selecting the materials that you'll use for a spell, those materials are chosen based on the nature of their indwelling spirits and the compatibility that exists among those spirits, knowing that nature is possible only through relationship with each spirit. This adds another step to the process of casting the spell, creating a ritual founded in animism as you connect with, for example, the unique spirit of a rose bush outside your home who, contrary to every correspondence list you can find, insists you cut this branch and burn the leaves to calm yourself and facilitate sympathy between you and other spirits.

Ritual is the basic structure of what you do, shaping the how of your magick and providing you a reliable and replicable course of action to take in response to various situations in which you'll find yourself as a witch. Ritual includes the foundational process behind casting a spell as much as it does the etiquette you follow when interacting with spirits or journeying to the Otherworld. Ritual is the familiarity in practice that brings comfort and results.

Spirit Work

Spirit work describes the nature of how the witch embodies their craft. It is animism in action, the ways in which we acknowledge the existence of the very many spirit people with whom we share the world and how we build relationships with them in the context of witchcraft. Spirit work is a broad term that refers to the interactions and relationships you have with spirits, as well as the skills that are necessary to have those interactions, build those relationships, and support yourself in that work.

Despite its ability to be a part of numerous magickal systems, spirit work is so integral to witchcraft that if you were to remove it, what you would be left with would not be recognizable as witchcraft from a historical, traditional, or even folkloric stance. The two are so inextricably entwined that there are few aspects of witchcraft that do not include spirits in some way. If it feels as if something is missing from your witchcraft practice, that missing piece is nearly always spirit work and, more specifically, *personal* relationships with spirits. We are not meant to be alone, and this is as true for us as living humans who need companionship and the support of community for our very survival as it is for us as witches who only ever discover just how much we are capable of—and how much is possible—in this craft once we are allied with a handful of spirits.

Through Practice and Application

As a practice, witchcraft is a toolkit for experiencing the world more fully for what it is and for more effectively operating within the reality it reveals to us. It provides us with a collection of skills and techniques whose use is guided by worldview (as worldview shapes the how's and why's of our actions). These skills not only help us to navigate that reality of living in a world filled with spirits and where changing energy currents influence our lives, but are also the foundation of how we work magick within this system.

It's important to note that skills can only be learned. One can be born with proclivity—the tendency to gravitate toward a certain activity or practice—but no one is born with skills. Your ability as a witch comes down entirely to the strength of your skills, and those skills must be deliberately cultivated and honed. The idea of "gifts" is a myth that creates division and a false sense of superiority, both of which stand in opposition to animism and are already far too prevalent within the witchcraft community. There is nothing innate to witchcraft that is sprinkled across humanity, appearing in some people but not others. The popular young adult literary theme of the chosen one remains an element of fiction and rooted in a worldview that is behind the rampant hyper individualism that has fostered such a strong sense of separation between us and the Land, between us and each other.

The only way to be a witch is to practice witchcraft. That is the only defining trait for what makes a witch. Even proclivity or natural talent cannot compete against practiced skill—it cannot compete against determined practice and focused effort on honing your skills to a knife's edge. Witchcraft is open to everyone. The ability to cultivate the necessary skills to practice witchcraft is available to us all—regardless of race, culture, gender, sexuality, age, able bodiedness, mental health, or neurodivergence. Nothing within these is a barrier to you practicing witchcraft: you just have to be willing to do the work.

In considering the wide range of skills that a witch may cultivate and hone throughout their career, there are seven skills that stand out as being foundational in that they can be built upon and are used continuously. Consciously working to develop these skills is how to practice witchcraft effectively and how to become a more competent witch; revisiting them from time to time can help you to ensure there are no gaps in your practice and to better see how far you've come since you first began practicing (which can be difficult to gauge without some sort of standard to compare against).

These seven foundational skills are:

- awareness

- discipline

- discernment

- energy work

- focus

- strength of Will

- visualization

Awareness

This is the ability to pay attention without expectations or judgment. It is a passive state of receptivity in which you experience what is there to be experienced, being open to the subtlety of spiritual forces (energy) within and without you. Awareness directly impacts your ability to feel energy and the presence of spirits, to have strong intuition, and to practice divination effectively. This is, to put it bluntly, your ability to be present physically and spiritually. It is a state of wholeness, where your physical body and spirit body work together.

Admittedly, awareness is a more difficult skill to develop than it comes across because it requires us to take whatever expectations we have about what "should" happen or how something is "supposed to" work and to put them to the side where they no longer influence our thoughts. It also means when we decide to do something (such as try a new spirit communication technique) we don't develop expectations as to what is supposed to happen—or what is or is not possible—before we've even had a chance to see what could happen, what might be possible. In this way, awareness relates to discipline because it is, in part, dependent upon being disciplined with our thoughts.

That lack of expectations is crucial because expectations create parameters for what we are able to experience. Sticking with our example of spirit communication, if you think that a spirit can only communicate with you in X way, when that spirit communicates with you in Y, Z, or A way, you may not notice or you may even dismiss what you're experiencing because it doesn't match your expectations of how things are "supposed to" go. Those expectations limit what you're able to experience in the moment and thus what you're capable of in that moment, too.

Discipline

Discipline is your ability to follow through: to identify a problem and then do the work necessary to solve it. When you first chose to become a witch and began practicing witchcraft, you likely decided upon a specific area or skill you wanted to learn. This may have been divination, candle magick, or the uses of stones. Regardless of what you chose, you became proficient in that area and developed those skills through discipline: by remaining focused and applying consistent effort until you achieved the results you wanted.

You didn't just suddenly come by that knowledge or skill because you called yourself a witch. You earned it by being in control of yourself, through your willingness to do things necessary to meet your goals and to your own benefit despite the challenges encountered. That's discipline.

Discipline is what gives you the ability to learn new skills, to be in control of energy, to work magick and to see results. It is your ability to discover how challenging witchcraft is and to keep pushing forward regardless of that difficulty. It is your ability to confront fear, complacency, to confront lack and boldly declare: "I can do better." Discipline is what empowers your Will because it is what justifies your confidence in your skills as a witch. It encompasses both applied curiosity and your willingness to *dare*: to do so for no reason than to see what might happen. It is a rite of passage within witchcraft that we all reach a point where things become inexplicably challenging: the excitement of being new to witchcraft wears off, that beautiful success rate your spells had begins to wane, and you can't help but feel that something is missing, that there is something more to all of this that exists outside of the tools and books you've collected. Discipline is how you respond when the bone deep call that brought you to witchcraft grows quiet. It's what keeps you searching for—and helps you to find—that special thing that proves to you that all your efforts have been worthwhile.

Discernment

Within witchcraft, discernment is both a skill and a practice. As a skill, it is your ability to tell *this* from *that*. It is how you know the difference between fluctuations in your energy levels and fluctuations you're feeling as a result of external energetic influence. It's how you know the difference between genuine spirit communication and wishful thinking or your imagination filling in the blanks. Without strong discernment skills, there will always be room for excessive doubt in your practice—as well as undue confidence. You cannot be competent or effective with weak discernment skills because discernment directly translates to your accuracy in interpreting the variety of sensations—spiritual and physical—that you experience in response to things like changes in the energy currents about you or the presence of a new spirit within your home.

As a practice, discernment relates to the skills of awareness and focus, as it is your ability to hold yourself in that state of objective awareness—without expectations or judgments—for the purpose of allowing insight to come through. Discernment is active contemplation; it uses the wandering of thoughts along a general route in order to encourage sudden insight and inspiration. More than overthinking, discernment is how you begin learning witchcraft from your firsthand experiences of doing witchcraft. It is how you pit the knowledge of courses and books (like this one!) against your personal experiences to find the truth they may—or may not—hold.

This form of discernment is how you gradually stop expecting witchcraft to behave logically and learn how it behaves through your observations (because logical conclusions relating to witchcraft typically follow no pattern pursuant to magick but, rather, tend to adhere to popular and/or influential ideas of the time, if not worldviews that hold magick to be the stuff of nonsense altogether). Discernment as a contemplative practice is how you begin shifting your worldview and making connections between ideas and experience that will increase your skill level.

Energy Work

Energy is the common term used (for better or worse) to refer to the subtle forces that lie at the heart of all magickal action. It is non-sentient; you cannot communicate with energy, it's not alive, it's not a being. It is inherently neutral—good/bad are not universal constructs, but instead cultural and personal, and so reframing them as "positive" or "negative" doesn't change this and has no bearing on the nature of energy. Ultimately, we have no idea what energy *is*. But we know there is something there, something that we can impact and that can impact us. We also know that we can do certain things and, as a result, more consistently and effectively impact that certain something. And so, we call that something energy because we have to give it a name in order to talk about it.

As witches, our work with energy takes two forms: sensing energy and manipulating energy. That manipulation of energy takes three general forms:

- push (project, repel)

- pull (attract, draw)

- or hold (contain)

Any type of magickal action you can think of will incorporate one, some, or all of these actions. If you are doing protection magick, such as creating a ward, you are pushing energy into a physical object that will then slowly dissipate that energy so as to repel unwanted energy and influence. If you are doing healing work, you will pull energy into you and then push that energy out of you to cause a desired effect in that person you are healing. If you are communicating with a spirit, you are gently extending your personal energy and then holding it in place to facilitate focused awareness of that spirit. If you are practicing energy exercises, you are very obviously pushing and pulling energy within and without yourself. Whatever type of magick you are working, the basic actions you are taking involve pushing, pulling, or holding energy.

As a result, your skill in energy manipulation naturally translates to greater skill and efficacy in all aspects of magick, including spellcraft, spirit communication, and divination.

Focus

Where awareness is passive and objective, focus is active and specific. In this way, they are sort of two sides of the same skill-coin. Focus is your ability to pay attention but with concentration applied to a purpose. When you cast a spell, focus is your ability to raise energy and direct it to its goal. When you walk across the land, focus is your ability to hold yourself alert yet receptive to your surroundings. It is also a critical skill specifically in spirit work as it is how you call to your ancestors, for example, and have only your ancestors show up and not random deceased humans. Focus is awareness with boundaries that allow you to achieve a desired goal based on your receptivity and sensitivity (to spiritual forces).

Focus also relates to discipline, as it is the difference between a witch who sees needed change, makes plans, and creates the change and a witch who talks about how spiritual they are but frequently has excuses as to why they can't actually practice witchcraft. Focus is the direction to which action and effort are applied, it's what helps you to stay on track with your studies as a witch and not become distracted by how much it feels like there is to learn—it keeps you on a path rather than going in circles.

Unfortunately, there is a lot against us all when it comes to strengthening focus. Our society strives to keep the pace of life racing by, with our thoughts necessarily racing and flitting by as a consequence. As a result, this can be one of the more difficult skills not just to learn but to use with consistency (at first). But "difficult" does not mean "impossible;" this is merely one of many challenges that lends support to the idea that to become a witch is to become something altogether different, something feral and existing at the edges of what is and what might be.

Strength of Will

Will—with deliberate capitalization—is the powering factor behind magick. While energy makes the magick go, it is your Will that takes hold of that energy, shapes it, and throws it at its target. It is the skill with which you transgress the order of the universe and create change that suits your goals, needs, and desires. The strength of your Will is impacted by your sense of self, your ability to know who you are, and to discern yourself from other influences and beings (which makes it related to and dependent upon, in some ways, your discernment skills).

Will is also impacted by your confidence in your skills as a witch. In this way, a strong sense of Will requires you to be honest with yourself about yourself and about your discipline regarding your witchcraft because it's easier to enact your Will when you know you are a capable and competent witch. And that knowledge comes through knowing you've done the work—and having the results of that work as proof—to show you that you are capable and competent.

Strong Will makes for faster and more potent results in magick. It's what lets you move past the tools and ritual to create change in your life with just a thought, what makes the use of magick reflexive and an extension of who you are at your core. But your Will is strengthened only through repetition and stubborn commitment to the idea that you are worthy and capable of wielding the forces of the universe—and that is discipline.

It's important to keep in mind that it takes time to develop Will. It involves a change of attitude that comes through consistent effort (remember: consistent doesn't mean constant but it does mean regularly). Will is the belief that you can take hold of the forces of the cosmos and use them to create change within it. Getting results helps to harden Will because those results remove the necessity of belief, instead replacing it with firm knowledge. You *will* work this magick, you will get the results you desire, because your Will is strong as a result of your efforts.

Visualization

Perhaps the most poorly named skill, visualization is a means of simulating spiritual sensations by recreating the accompanying physical sensations through your mind. This is a way for you to train yourself to experience those sensations so that you can, for example, more easily feel the presence of a spirit and see them before you (in a sort of layering of mental imagery over top the physical, in a way that means you can sometimes see a spirit before you through closed eyes), or feel your ancestors around you and hear them offer guidance toward a challenge you're facing.

Full sensory recreation is what distinguishes visualization, as a potent magickal exercise and tool, from that of make believe or daydreaming. This is an important distinction because real magick isn't happening just in your head. It is the cooperation of your mind, your physical body, and your spirit body to effectively wield energy that is essential to work magick. Take one of those things out of the equation and you're just going through the motions.

That full recreation includes not just imagery but also any relevant sensations you would experience through your other senses, such as smell and sound. It also includes things like the twisting of your gut in response to the emotion a situation you're visualizing holds, or visualizing a favorite food and feeling the rushing of blood across your skin in response to the increase of psychic sensitivity that comes with the desire felt when seeing that food. In truth, re-creating imagery can be a starting point for visualization, but it is not the primary concern and successful visualization can be done with no visual recreation.

Try not to approach visualization as something that you have to be able to do to completion every time, recreating sensory information as if you're crossing items off a list. Rather, focus on the dominant sensory details, sinking yourself into the experience and gently moving yourself closer to full recreation. This will be far more beneficial—both in the short term and the long term.

Understanding Worldview

Worldview is the fundamental perception of the world that influences how one thinks about the world and how one moves through the world; it affects how you see yourself, how you see others, how you treat yourself, how you treat others, and how you justify those thoughts and actions.

If you were to distill the basic motivation for your actions along a dominant theme, that theme would be your worldview. It is the definitive flavor of your thoughts and your actions, the explanation for the way that you do things and how you relate to others. It is how you see the world, why you see things that way; it's how you think about how you see things, it's the basis of your values, it influences your priorities. Worldview informs everything you think and do.

All religions are founded upon a distinct worldview, but a worldview can be shared among various cultures; animism is a perfect example of a worldview that is shared among a variety of differing religions and cultures while remaining evident within that unique cultural context.

In addition to animism, there are four basic worldviews that tend to be discussed within the context of witchcraft. These worldviews are:

- monotheism
- pantheism
- panentheism
- polytheism

Monotheism

The belief that there exists one singular deity Who exists within and separate from the physical world. As a worldview, it frequently goes hand in hand with dualism, which posits a separation between the physical and the spiritual, including a separation between living humans and that deity, as well as between living humans and the dead. Dualism stands in stark contrast and opposition to animism. Emphasis is placed on being in right relationship with that singular deity so that one can be with them in death.

Pantheism

The belief that "the divine" or "god" exists in all things and that physicality is the manifestation of "the divine." Rather than unique and individual spirits within all things, there is part of a greater divine whole that is present in all things; that divine essence does not exist outside of Its presence in physical matter nor in an individual manner. Emphasis is placed on living from a place of awareness of that divine immanence in oneself and others.

Panentheism

Similar to pantheism, panentheism differs in that the divine is believed to be both imminent (within all physicality) and transcendent (existing separate to physicality and in an individual manner). Emphasis is placed on living in awareness of the divine in all things and in such a way so as to encourage transcendence for the individual, with the form of that transcendence varying based on personal belief. As a term, it was coined in the 18th century to distinguish it, as a philosophy, from pantheism (which had arisen barely a hundred years prior).

Polytheism

Also called theism, this is the belief in the existence of many, living, complex, individual, and autonomous deities Who exist within and without the physical world and Whose presence and actions maintain order in the cosmos. Emphasis is placed on living one's life so as to be in right relationship with these deities. Polytheism and animism are not exactly the same thing but frequently go hand in hand and are complementary to each other. Like animism, polytheism is ancient yet still quite prevalent throughout the world.

Exercises

Throughout this book, you will find a number of exercises to complete with each lesson. They are designed to help you take the material you've read and internalize it through contemplation and direct experience. The exercises will be different in each lesson, though you can generally expect there to be a combination of journaling—to help guide your thoughts—and activities to help you build skill and act within the context of animism.

For this lesson, you will be journaling and performing an energy exercise. Each exercise should take about twenty to thirty minutes to complete. In addition to the following journal prompt, you may wish to record your thoughts about or any questions you had while reading this lesson. Remember that you do not have to complete the exercises in one shot, you are welcome to split them up, completing them on separate days and fitting them into your schedule as best works for you.

Exercise 1: Identifying Worldview—Journal Prompt

After looking at the defining traits of witchcraft, and the foundational skills this craft entails, consider the ways that witchcraft impacts your worldview. How does your witchcraft practice affect the way that you think? How does your witchcraft practice affect the ways you perceive the world? How does your witchcraft impact the way that you interact with the world around you?

Let your thoughts wander and allow these questions to be as expansive as possible. There are no right or wrong answers: there is only the unique way that witchcraft is shaping you—and your life.

You can approach this exercise however you feel comfortable. If you find words pouring forth from you, amazing. If you find yourself making single word lists across the page in response to each question, perfect. There are no "right" answers (only *your answers) and there is no right form for your responses.*

Exercise 2: Scavenger Hunt—Energy Exercise

For this exercise you will need to gather a collection of objects from about your home. Ideally, you will need:

- one man-made object (for example, your favorite coffee cup, a family heirloom, your favorite Tarot deck)

- one inanimate natural object (a stone you found in your front yard, a smooth stick from the park)

- one animate object (a plant or pet)

Assemble your items before you. Now, you're going to attempt to feel the energy within each object. You can use your hands, face, feet, or whole body to do this; you may notice different results depending on what body part you use, so don't be afraid to experiment.

Begin by turning your attention to that object. Now get closer to it; this could be by holding your hand or foot over it, holding your face near to it, or holding the object and drawing it near to your chest. Focus your attention lightly on the object and pay attention to all sensations you experience—spiritual, emotional, and physical. For example, you might (but might not) feel a tingle in the part of your body closest to the object, you may have an impression of different colors in your mind, or your body may suddenly feel warmer or colder.

What sensations you experience doesn't matter so much as you notice the subtle ways that you, personally, respond in relation to your proximity to that object. Different types of sensations do not mean anything, what sensations you experience do not reflect anything inherent to the object: they are different ways that you are responding to spiritual/energetic stimuli.

Record your observations and then repeat the exercise with your remaining objects.

Now you're going to repeat this exercise, however, you're going to center yourself before you attempt to feel the energy of each object.

Centering is a technique that reorients you within yourself. It seats your awareness more fully within yourself and brings your seat of consciousness more fully into your physical being (which helps you to be more aware of what's going on within and without you).

> To center, sit comfortably with your spine as straight as you can comfortably manage. Close your eyes and relax your breathing. You can breathe in for a count of four and exhale for a count of five, or similar, if you wish.
>
> Focus on your breathing. You will notice that your attention naturally turns inward. Feel through that darkness behind your closed eyes, gently feeling where your attention is moving toward. Feel the immensity of that blackness. Feel the way every inhalation creates that immensity within you. But as vast and expansive as you are in that place, you still remain at the center of it. As

limitless as the boundaries about you feel, there you still are: at the center, firm and unmoving.

Continue to breathe, holding yourself at that center point, at the point where your spirit body and physical body are one and the same, at that point where you and the cosmos meet and are connected.

Now attempt to feel the energy in each object again, using your hands, feet, face, body, all three, or a combination thereof. Record your observations.

Some things to consider as you reflect on your experiences and that you may find useful to record in your notes: How do these two experiences compare—feeling energy without centering and with centering? How do they contrast? Were there similarities with the same objects? Were there similarities in whether you centered beforehand? Were there similarities depending on what part of your body you used to feel the energy?

While there are no right or wrong answers, it can be beneficial to have a record of your experience so you can revisit this exercise in the future and compare your experiences. This can be a great way to see how your skills have improved and the ways that you are growing as a witch.

Final Note

Witchcraft affords us an opportunity to establish connections between ourselves and the variety of beings with whom we share the world. Not only does it show us firsthand the vast array of spirit beings that exist around us, but it provides us the tools necessary to better navigate that reality—helping us to be in right relationship with those spirits. We covered a lot in this lesson: establishing a shared definition of witchcraft, identifying the foundational skills of this craft, exploring the ways that worldview impacts all aspects of our lives, and applying some of those foundational skills (specifically awareness, discernment, energy work, and focus) to begin experiencing the world in the way that witchcraft strives to reveal it to us. It's only our first lesson, but already you are taking important steps to more fully embracing animism—steps that you will build upon and that will help you to continue to see results from your efforts.

Lesson 2

Witchcraft Comes from the Land

Animism is an ongoing effort to be in right relationship with those around us, thus creating an interlocking web of relationships that form the basis of community. To sink ourselves more deeply into animism is to sink ourselves more deeply into the web of relationships and the web of community, binding ourselves to those around us through mutual awareness, respect, and obligation. In this way, animism—like any worldview—cannot be practiced. It is not a religion, not a system: it is a way of existing within the world. It can only be lived, defining every action the witch takes—be it those actions specifically focused on the everyday or upon the spiritual.

If animism describes the nature of the witch, then the Land describes the nature of witchcraft. And where the Land and the witch intersect, spirit work describes the nature of how the witch embodies their craft. Again and again, it all comes down to the Land, the very source of witchcraft, and the actions we take to be aware of and responsive to the existence and the autonomy it possesses. Yet the Land is not "Mother Nature." It is not an impersonal archetype nor is it a resource for us to exploit and use. The Land—as a physical place intersecting with the world of spirits and overlaid with our personal experiences and interpretations—is a dynamic and fluid space, one that is ever changing, ever becoming. It is as receptive as it is assertive. In our relationships with the land and its many spirits, this imposes upon us obligation to approach those relationships as also being alive, requiring tending and demanding certain actions and behaviors from us.

Understanding Animism

Witchcraft a system that is dependent upon the awareness of and interaction with spiritual forces and beings. Because of its awareness of and use of spiritual forces, this naturally shows us that it, too, is dependent upon some type of worldview—one that encompasses the existence of a variety of spiritual forces and beings. These spiritual forces are typically called energy and these spiritual beings are typically called spirits, and both can be found within objects, such as the energy of a stone, as well as outside of objects, such as the spirits of your ancestors.

While these two things—energy and spirits—can seem like radical concepts within Western society, they are concepts intrinsic to animism.

It's important to remember that, ultimately, we have no idea what energy is. It is not the energy discussed in any branch of science, and it is unable to currently be sensed or measured except through the use of spiritual skills—which makes its existence impossible to prove to anyone but ourselves. Yet we know that something is there. If you put in the time and effort to develop strong psychic/spiritual skills, you will have experiences that corroborate the existence of energy for you. And in those experiences, you can find similarities with the experiences of other witches who have likewise developed those skills.

Thus over the course of the last seventy years, during which time contemporary witchcraft has been born and proliferated throughout the world, there is a vast collection of experiences that—despite the inability to say much about energy with certainty—provide us a general standard of how energy behaves and how it can be affected, as well as providing us a general standard of what to expect when feeling and moving energy. Because of this, we are able to discern suitable actions to take in order to cultivate the skills necessary to effectively sense and manipulate energy.

Animism holds that the world is alive with spirits. That's the simple definition, but in practice, the waters of animism flow deep. In a world that is alive and thrumming with spirits, the place of humans can be summed up as one among many. Contrasting— and conflicting—with the dominant worldview of Euro-American Christianized society (that often prizes the individual over community), this means that humans do not exist in superiority to any spirit. We are not special in relation to the vast number of other beings that exist within the cosmos alongside us.

There is no hierarchy among the variety of beings that exist— be they physical or spirit. Humans are not better than spirits regardless if those spirits are human dead, animal dead, the spirit in a mountain, the spirit in a river, a wandering spirit caught in your home, or the spirit within your coffee maker.

The term "spirit" refers to a spectrum of beings that are generally comprised of energy. Spirits are not "ghosts." There exists as much variety in spirits as there does physical expressions of being; human dead are just one type of spirit that exists, and they exist as a very small percentage.

Some spirits exist with physical form (such as the spirits of plants or stones), some spirits once had physical form and now do not (such as human and animal dead), and some spirits have never had physical form nor will they likely ever have physical form (of which there is a large variety of spirits, such as the Good Folk, trolls, and the Gods). While spirits exist primarily in energetic form, all energy is not a spirit nor does it emanate from a spirit (we'll expound upon this in Lesson 3: A World Alive with Spirits).

As a term, "ghost" can be viewed as infantilizing, as it focuses upon creating and maintaining separation between the living and the dead. This is problematic for many reasons, such as the way that it strips personhood from the dead and discourages viewing other spirits as possessing personhood, the way that it eliminates our accountability to the dead, the way that it creates an illusion of power that we hold over the dead and thus death (thereby enforcing hierarchy among beings and centering living humans), and the way that it further encourages us to fear death and, as a result, our own physicality.

These things contrast sharply against animism and are generally not compatible with the way that animism asks us to perceive ourselves, perceive other beings (that is, as people), and perceive ourselves in relation to other people. This serves as a good example of the surprising ways that worldview influences our thoughts, our perceptions, and behavior as we see that the concept of ghosts is largely embedded in a worldview dependent upon separation and maintaining so much of the pain that we try to dissolve and heal as animists.

What is special, however, is the connection that exists between us and these spirits (and, as a result, all other humans—living and dead—and all animals and all insects and all plants and the Earth and . . .). It is the existence of relationship between us and these spirits that is the focus of animism. This is the way that animism influences and changes our behavior, because we have an obligation as animists to be in right relationship with spirits as much as any physically incarnate being. Animism demands that we prize community and that we recognize that community absolutely includes our local spirits as much as it includes our fellow humans and other forms of physical beings.

Underpinning that recognition is the awareness and acknowledgment that every spirit exists as its own autonomous being. These beings are not part of any larger whole; rather, each spirit is unique and complete, as much an individual as you or me. We'll go into the concept of personhood of spirits in more detail in Lesson 3: A World Alive with Spirits.

As you're likely beginning to notice, despite animism being frequently defined as the "belief that all things have a spirit," this definition does little to demonstrate the far reaching influence animism has on someone nor does it describe how that person experiences the world. It's an imperfect definition, reductive and dismissive. Such a statement implies that a declaration of belief is enough to be an animist.

So, we will instead focus on understanding animism through three defining traits that deeply relate to each other and gradually demonstrate how animism will be evident in your actions if it is your worldview. As we noted earlier, your worldview influences how you think, how you behave, and how you experience everything. It is impossible for your worldview to not show in your actions.

These three defining traits are:

· lack of separation

· diversity is the nature of the cosmos

· right relationship and community

As can only be expected with animism, these three traits cannot be cleanly separated. And so, you will see a strong connection among them all because animism is not about separation but wholeness. Where most of the other worldviews we discussed—specifically Christian monotheism, pantheism, and panentheism—largely focus on linear progression and rise and fall, animism is focused on interconnection, webs of relationship, and cycles. And so, we will be diving into these traits throughout this book via their interconnection, approaching them from individual threads that then weave themselves together to show how fully adopting animism as a worldview can change your life.

Without the Land, There Is No Witchcraft

Similar to how situating yourself into the current of a deity causes you to become more like Them, rooting yourself to the land—to a specific local place—causes you to exhibit traits that demonstrate your belonging to that place because you become infused with the energy of that location. This is very much in line with the process of inscendence as coined by Thomas Berry. Inscendence is the opposite of transcendence. It describes the process of sinking into the land, of seeking the core of the world and becoming so beautifully tangled up with the heart of it, with life and living.

> Inscendence is the process of entangling ourselves with the Land, of establishing ourselves as belonging to our local land and as participating within the web of community that exists across the landscape. Where transcendence is a process of going above and existing separate to the physical world, inscendence is a process of sinking back into the source; as physical beings, our very existence comes from the land and it is to the land we will return in death.
>
> As stated by Thomas Berry in his work Evening Thoughts: Reflecting on Earth as Sacred Community:
>
> If we will the future effectively it will be because the guidance and the powers of the Earth have been communicated to us, not because we have determined the future of the Earth simply with some rational faculty.

In our context, inscendence is the process of entangling the witch with the Land, of seating yourself as one who is recognized by the local land spirits as belonging to that location; land-based witchcraft only means "local practice." For obvious reasons, one cannot state that they belong to a location—asserting that you do, and you're not Indigenous to that location, is a very good indicator that you do not belong. Much like the term ally is a title that is bestowed upon a spirit in recognition of the close relationship you have with them, belonging to the Land is a condition solely determined by those specific local land spirits and/or the Indigenous peoples of that place. Achieving that belonging is not simple nor is it quick.

Already, you have likely noticed places where the concept of animism is grating against your current worldview. There may be some aspects of animism that feel uncomfortable; you may even find yourself becoming angry in response to some of the things you've read. This discomfort is important to acknowledge because it demonstrates how great the process of embracing animism is— how it is an ongoing effort to peel back the layers of influence that Euro-American society has impressed upon you, seeing the way each layer encourages you to center yourself over other humans, to center the experience and preferences of living humans over all other beings. And so, it takes considerable effort to remove enough of that influence to where the separation that exists between you and the Land can begin to be resolved.

Or, perhaps, you feel as if you finally have words to describe your worldview. You may feel joy and amazement that there's a term that describes what you've always known to be true. You may even feel more strongly connected to the land, to its spirits, and to other humans knowing that this worldview—your worldview— isn't just the oldest worldview known to humans but remains one of the most common ways of experiencing the world, too.

Alive with Spirits

When we speak of the Land, it is the physical land—a specific location and space—in conjunction with the countless spirits that exist within that landscape to which we are referring. This designation is important because, as animists, it acknowledges the layers of obligation and responsibility that exist for us. It reminds us of that quality of Other, that existence of a unique spirit within each thing we encounter, and it reminds us to slow down, to act deliberately, to act with awareness of how we might affect each spirit.

Witchcraft exists as spiritual interplay between ourselves and the Land. It exists within that connection, enlivened by it, dependent upon it. As much as there is no craft of the witch without the witch, there is no witchcraft without the Land. Every object that we use for our magick, every component to any spell, comes from the land. Even the knowledge of how to practice this craft comes from the Land, as the spirits that you encounter can teach you techniques that do not exist in any book; they can teach you uses for those physical objects that defy any correspondence list you might come across. There is nothing of value regarding the inherent nature and practice of witchcraft that cannot be learned directly from the Land.

> There is no spiritual connection with the Land without a physical connection to the land. Intention without action means nothing in witchcraft nor in life; it is our actions that reveal our character and our priorities. Without a physical connection to the land—without knowledge and interaction with the land upon which you live—a spiritual connection is impossible. When we speak of land spirits, it is not some monolith of spirits to which we are referring, it is not a nebulous force of energy that can be tapped into and manipulated. These are not archetypes. We are only speaking of individual and

> unique spirits with whom you share the land, whom you encounter
> every day of your life. When we speak of relationships with these
> spirits, it is your direct interactions with them and the efforts you
> are taking to be in right relationship with them. These are not
> unknowable beings, these spirits are people that you are able to
> meet, to know, to ally with, to learn witchcraft directly from.

One of the things that sets witchcraft apart and sometimes serves as a stumbling point is its heavy focus on the physical world and everyday life. The goal of the witch is not to escape life, to attain godhead, or to transcend the physical world. It is inscendence, to become entangled with the Land and thoroughly embroiled in witchcraft. And we can see this entanglement directly translate to a focus on common aspects of human life and ways that we can make our lives better for ourselves. What is the obsession with love spells but a human need for connection and support? What is the relevance of prosperity magick but an effort to make our lives easier so that we are better able to appreciate the joy of living and being physically incarnate?

And so, the work we do (and the work—the doing of witch-craft—is the point of it all) serves to further anchor us within phys-icality, allowing us to meet an incredible variety of spirits on equal terms and to achieve inscendence—where we entangle ourselves with the Land, with life, with living.

With Change Comes Challenge

As we've already explored, animism is the oldest and most perva-sive worldview among humans. It is important to remember, however, that animism is not a religion. Nor is it something that can be practiced. Rather, animism is an all encompassing way of being that affects you not just as a witch, but also in the way that you live your life. This means that it naturally conflicts with other ways of being, other worldviews.

In moving from the place where you are learning about animism to living as an animist, it is important to realize the false dichotomy of the above statement (that is, animism affecting you as a witch and in the way you live your life). There is no separation between magick and the mundane, between the physical and the spiritual, between witchcraft and the rest of your life. However, this is a difficult concept to incorporate into your life—partly why it is mentioned so frequently within discussions of witchcraft among practitioners.

A consequence of living in Western society, and within a culture whose worldview is largely based upon that of white evangelical Christianity, means that animism is a wholly alien concept to many of us, one that is at odds with the worldview in which we may have been raised. Even if you were not raised Christian, it is likely that it has influenced your life in some way because its presence within Western society is so strong. No one who has been raised within Euro-American society has escaped its influence, for better or worse, just like not one single white person in the West has escaped being raised within a mindset of coloniality. This doesn't mean that all people have had the same experience under a Christian-dominant society. Just as diversity is the nature of the cosmos, so is it also among humans. Christian Euro-American society, however, has homogenized our differences in ways that privilege one group in unearned ways at the expense of everyone who becomes "other." The Land and the web of spirits around us are categorized as the latter, and subjected to ideologies of control and dominion, similarly to people who are marginalized under this structure.

This influence means that becoming an animist is a process for many of us. We start in a place where we believe there is a distinction between magick and the mundane, between the physical and the spiritual, between witchcraft and the rest of our lives, due largely in part to our society's obsession with compartmentalization. Slowly, we move into believing there is no separation, yet animism remains a belief we need to remind ourselves of and purposely act upon so that we consistently have experiences that support that belief. And then we finally live that lack of separation, having adopted the worldview of animism more fully. It is a process. Any progress you make in unraveling your worldview and embracing animism is to be celebrated, because it is difficult; there is encouragement from every angle of the dominant overculture to not make that progress, to choose oneself over community.

The way that we understand the land has a lot to do with who we are and the influences we carry with us. Factors such as culture, age, and class affect the ways that we perceive the land and contribute to the experiences we have and are capable of having with the land in ways that aren't always readily apparent to us, especially if those factors create unspoken power dynamics between us and others. Who we are sets parameters for what we are able to experience because it informs the expectations, judgments, and preconceived notions we hold that directly limit what we are able to experience (in relation to the land) in a spiritual capacity—which is not to dismiss the social factors that can, and do, create very real limitations and specific circumstances surrounding what we have, can, and do experience in relation to the land.

This highlights the importance of going slowly, making the time to challenge our assumptions and to dig into areas where we encounter discomfort and frustration. This is essential for us to learn to decenter ourselves, to release assumptions that everyone shares our experiences, and to not act as if our personal experiences, preferences, and viewpoints are the default experiences, preferences, and views—an attitude that becomes essential in forming relationships with spirits but must also be held in regard to other living humans. This also highlights how, even when you're not doing witchcraft, the attitude and thought processes that inform the practice of witchcraft (that is, animism) are evident in your everyday actions.

In considering that witchcraft, as we are defining and approaching it here, is ultimately a toolkit for dissolving separation and attaining wholeness within ourselves (as we'll explore in Lesson 5: The Layered Witch) and with the Land (as we'll explore in Lesson 6: The Layered World), it is meaningful for us to note the growing body of evidence that shows that a strong attachment to the natural world, particularly your local land, holds direct benefit to your health—physical, mental, and emotional—and that severing that connection has noticeable adverse effects on well-being. As much as there are challenges in adopting the worldview of animism, your efforts to do so will yield results. Your efforts will gradually begin to create a new foundation for your witchcraft, one that is rooted in the Land, founded on personal relationships, and that minimizes some of the pain that comes as a result of living in separation from the land and the spirit world.

Exercises

In working to develop—and then hone—foundational skills in witchcraft, repetition is crucial. When doing an exercise for the first time, it's not unusual to find yourself utilizing your physical body and your spirit body, together, in a way that you may never have before. That first attempt can be filled with uncertainty, and it can be rather awkward and full of stumbles. This makes trying again so very important, as you can build off that first attempt. Even a "failed" first attempt has value as now you're aware of where things might not have gone quite right, where things felt confusing, and where the desire to do it right and have the right experience might have gotten in your way.

With continued practice, you figure out how to make your physical body and spirit body work together smoothly, allowing you to apply your developing skills in your witchcraft—helping you to see how those skills work in practice and how they are used throughout witchcraft.

For this reason, this lesson includes three exercises, along with encouragement to go back and revisit the energy sensitivity exercise you practiced in Exercise 2: Scavenger Hunt of the previous lesson. Repetition will make it easier to feel energy on command, and it's a crucial first step in being able to feel the presence of spirits—and communicate with them.

The third exercise is a long-term one, but do try to make some progress on it now, as it will be easier to manage if broken into small blocks of time. Try to spend about twenty to thirty minutes on each exercise; the ongoing exercise of practicing feeling energy in objects and beings can be done a few minutes at a time and spontaneously throughout your day, making it easier to make multiple attempts as you work through this lesson.

Exercise 1: Identifying Obstacles and Opportunities— Journal Prompt

Now that you have a better idea of what animism is and how it can impact the way you live your life, take some time to look at your life and be really honest with yourself about the things that you are doing—your actions and the way you live your life—that are in line with an animist worldview. You can freewrite, letting your thoughts wander, or even make a list of words and phrases. Try to list at least three things.

Being completely honest with yourself, now identify some of the most glaring ways that you are not living as an animist and the most striking aspects of your thought processes and basic views that conflict with animism. This list is not meant to make you feel guilty or that you aren't doing enough, it is meant to show you where discrepancies lie and where you may be the most resistant to adopting a new worldview.

To build off of this, and keeping in mind that animism is a worldview and thus can only be seen through one's actions, identify three ways that you can start living animism—in addition to the ways that you already identified as things you already are doing. These could be extensions of those things, ways that you are taking them further, but try to list at least one new thing.

Now to take this one step further. Consider what the major obstacles are that you face in adopting an animist worldview. You can freewrite or create a list of words and phrases, again, or you could experiment with a mind map, noting major obstacles, smaller obstacles that influence them, and the connections that exist among those obstacles. There may be crossover with this list and the second list you made, in regard to thought processes and views.

Try to give yourself time to consider why each obstacle exists, how it affects you, and—most importantly—what steps to removing this obstacle could look like. Don't worry if you are only able to list a few obstacles or if you have a list that surprises you in length. The point is to get you to start thinking about what your life is like now—what your thoughts, current relationships, habits, are like—and how that differs from what you imagine your life, having fully embraced an animist worldview, could be like. It's also important to note that some of the obstacles you list could be systemic in nature, leaving little or no options for you in terms of personal action to remove them or ability to find safe workarounds. Noting these obstacles can serve as a reminder that there is no way to be an animist and not exist in the world that we have been given. Solutions come through communal action. It is not your responsibility to solve every possible obstacle that exists before you—nor is it your fault that those obstacles exist in the first place. This speaks directly to the pressures placed on BIMPOC (Black, Indigenous, Mixed People of Color) individuals especially.

Revisit this list and modify it as necessary as you work through this book. Add new things that you realized you were doing that are already animistic. Remove some obstacles as you work through them. Realize connections—some obstacles aren't nearly as formidable as they might have initially felt.

This may be a challenging exercise and may bring up complicated and messy emotions. It's okay to work through this exercise slowly, allowing your emotions their time to rise and fall as you gently consider current realities and future possibilities. Remember that the emphasis of animism on recognizing our connections to others and acting with awareness of that connection includes allowing yourself to be supported and cared for, the emphasis of treating all beings with respect includes respecting—and taking care—of yourself. Allow yourself the grace of going slowly when you need to.

Exercise 2: Push and Pull—Energy Exercise

Energy work is the basis of spellcraft, but it is also critical in all other areas of witchcraft (hence why feeling and manipulating energy was listed as one of the foundational witchcraft skills in Lesson 1: Witchcraft and Worldview). Although energy and spirits are not the same thing, the skills used in feeling and manipulating energy are the same skills used to sense the presence of spirits and communicate with them—especially in regard to being able to discern their communication as originating outside of ourselves and not mistaking our own internal voice, thoughts, imagination, or desires for communication from a spirit as genuine spirit communication.

For this exercise, you will build off your growing experience in sensing energy, taking those skills further by raising and directing energy. As intimidating as that can sound, this is a very basic exercise and is generally easily learned. Nonetheless, it is a different way of experiencing the world than you may be used to, so it may take a few tries before the movements come naturally.

Sit comfortably with your spine as straight as is comfortable for you. Close your eyes and focus on your breathing. Perform the

Centering Exercise as detailed in Exercise 2: Scavenger Hunt of the previous lesson.

> Deliberately altering the pattern of your breathing can affect your blood pressure, causing it to lower or even drop. Depending on your health concerns, you may wish to arrange pillows around you for comfort or in case your blood pressure drops suddenly and you pass out. You may find better results with any sort of breath work and energy exercises if you perform them based upon your medication schedule. However, breath work, such as in centering, may pose additional risk for other chronic health concerns, such as a risk of seizure. It can also be triggering for those with C-PTSD, PTSD, or who are currently working through past traumatic experiences.
>
> Absolutely alter any exercise in this book as necessary for your safety. If an exercise inadvertently presents a risk to you, it is not necessary to complete it as written. Your safety and well-being matter more.
>
> For this exercise, all that is necessary to complete it is the focus on raising energy, directing it, and then taking the energy back into you. Everything else is optional but listed for the way that it can facilitate the core action and purpose of this exercise.

Open your eyes and raise your hands before your chest, palms together as if in prayer. Rub them together and gently stretch your fingers to warm your hands. Put your hands together again, palm to palm. Tense the muscles in your hands for a moment. As you do, begin focusing on pulling energy from within your core and moving it down through your arms and out of your hands. It can be helpful to visualize the energy, as focusing on creating the sensory sensations of moving energy can help to bridge the gap in skill and facilitate moving that energy through you. As part of your visualization, you may feel a sensation of water or wind moving down your arms, you may "see" the energy move in blue waves or lightning bolts. Feel free to experiment, to play off any sensations you may already be feeling, or to expand on any imagery that naturally comes to mind.

Cup your hands, separating them slightly so you can see between them, and focus on keeping the energy between your palms. At this stage, it can be helpful to visualize the energy moving between your hands as blue or white energy, similar to what you may see if you imagine electricity, moving out of your hands and forming a spinning ball of energy.

Continue to focus on pushing more energy down your arms and out through the palms of your hands. Separate your hands further as you continue to push the energy, so that they are no longer touching.

Now, bring your hands together slowly so you can feel the resistance. Separate your hands again as you push the energy out, focusing it into that ball shape still. Raise your hands to your face and slowly open your hands, allowing the energy ball to return to you, being absorbed into your face; rest your hands upon your face and pause for a moment, just breathing and feeling.

You may wish to record your experience, noting the different sensations you felt while pushing the energy as well as while bringing it back into you. This exercise can be readily adapted to a variety of situations (as it is that basic: projecting energy from your hands and pulling it towards and into you), so feel free to experiment with it. Be sure to record your results so you can begin identifying the boundaries of what is or is not possible with it, as well as potential applications where you can tell results are feasible but require more practice from you.

Outline of Steps

1. Sit in a way that is comfortable for you, close your eyes, and center yourself.

2. Open your eyes and bring your palms together before your chest.

3. Rub your hands together and stretch your fingers.

4. Place your hands palm to palm again, tense the muscles for a moment, and focus on moving energy from your core down your arms and out through your hands.

5. Cup your hands and separate them slightly so that there is some space between them.

6. Continue to focus on projecting energy out through your hands. Focus on the energy forming a glowing ball between your hands.

7. Push more energy into the ball and move your hands apart slightly to accommodate its larger size.

8. Bring your hands closer together and feel the slight resistance.

9. Separate your hands again, continuing to focus on maintaining that glowing ball of energy.

Alive with Spirits

10. Bring your hands to your face and gently pull the energy back into you through your face.

11. Rest your hands on your face and pause, just breathing and feelings.

12. Record your experiences and any sensations you felt during this exercise.

Exercise 3: Becoming a Local Witch

To be an animist and a witch is to cultivate relationships with the spirits with whom you share your local landscape and centering those relationships within your witchcraft practice. In this way, your practice becomes the embodiment of your worldview and these relationships—it becomes a demonstration of the ways in which you belong to that location on a physical and spiritual level.

Land-based practice means local practice. To help you better entangle yourself with your local land, for this exercise you will be actively discovering and learning about your local land—and discovering how to use that knowledge to support building relationships with your local land spirits so those relationships can better become the foundation of your witchcraft practice.

Choose three to five plants that you commonly see in your local area. These should be plants that you normally encounter without going out of your way to see them. That may mean that they are growing in your yard, you pass them on your way to work, or you encounter them when you visit a local park.

Identify and uncover as much information about each plant as you can. Learn the Latin name of each plant you've selected and the various common names by which they are known. Find out if they are native to where you live or if they were introduced. Many plants, such as dandelions and alfalfa, were deliberately introduced to North America and have become naturalized. If that plant was introduced, find out why. Were they used as food? Fodder? A clothing dye? Medicine for common complaints?

Identify any folklore, superstitions, or folk tales that accompany the plant. Are there any known medicinal or food uses for them? For plants native to the so-called Americas, search out uses by Indigenous peoples, as Eurocentric herbalism books often dismiss these plants as useless or having no proven benefit or use.

With many "European plants," a little extra digging may reveal that they, too, are not native and had been introduced from Asia and Africa and have longstanding traditional use among the peoples of those regions. Keep in mind there is no such thing as general or universal associations for any plant. Rather, there are stories and traditions that come from distinct peoples and cultures: don't be afraid to seek out details in place of white washed history and appropriation. The details matter.

What relationships does that plant have? Which pollinators does it feed? What other wildlife relies on it as a food source? What about other plants, do some grow better when near it? Does it grow better when near to particular other plants? What effect does it have on the soil? What does it need from the soil?

Now do the same for three to five trees that are growing in your area, as well.

This is an ongoing project; as you make progress and begin interacting with the individual spirits within specific plants of those species types (which we'll cover in future lessons), look for ways that you can engage these plants in your practice right now. And then do so. These plants are more in tune with the local energy currents and are, thus, able to more easily affect change within those currents—which means faster and more potent results for your magick.

Be creative and look for new ways that you can incorporate those plants into your life to aid you. Include them in a sachet. Make an oil and anoint yourself daily or before bed. If they're edible, include them in your meals. Bitter tasting roots, chopped, work great in soups and bean dishes; green tasting plants work well as teas, in foods with a lot of cheese, and in salads; any leaves without spines work well on pizza. Look for ways that keep you or your goal (as appropriate to the specific work) saturated in that plant's energy or ways that allow its energy more access to that which you seek to change. You can even make a practice of observing the plant's behavior and growth, perhaps every day for a week, perhaps throughout one growing cycle.

While there is a difference between the energy of a plant and the spirit of a plant, infusing your life with the energy of a specific plant species can help prepare you for interacting with the spirit of an individual plant of that species, making it easier for you to hear their voice and perhaps build a relationship with them.

Ongoing Exercises

Continue to practice feeling the energy of various objects and living beings. Remember to focus on feeling the energy of that object or being and not to focus on sensing the spirit within it. These are not the same thing and your ability to tell the difference (and to also be deliberate and focused with what you're doing as a witch) are necessary for the level of competency required for you to develop and maintain true relationships with various spirits, allowing you to call them ally and even friend.

Final Note

Animism emphasizes our connection to the land by demonstrating our dependency upon it for every aspect of witchcraft. The materials in our spells—be they dried herbs and resins, beeswax candles, red thread, or rusty iron nails—all come from the land. And our ability to manipulate those objects, as well as to manipulate energy, is dependent upon our own physical nature. We are not spirits having a physical experience, rather we are physical body and spirit body together. The cooperation of both are as essential for a joyful life as they are for effective witchcraft.

Yet true respect and appreciation for the land does not exist without involvement in your local area. Respect for the land and its spirits is little more than empty words without interacting with the land upon which you live and the spirits with whom you share that land. By making the effort to establish ourselves as belonging to the land, we may find the Land reaching up to embrace us—helping us to discover new ways of working magick that are based in our local energy currents, supported by relationships with our local spirits, and that rely upon materials gotten from our local land and techniques learned from local spirits.

Lesson 3

A World Alive with Spirits

The worldview of animism takes time to fully embody because with each layer of your current worldview peeled back, another area is revealed wherein the influence of our society has created sticking points and incompatibility in your thoughts and behaviors to that of animism. Recognizing and then working through those sticking points is ongoing work, frequently requiring you to revisit certain points as you discover new layers and sticking points that weren't apparent before. Yet this is the work that awaits any of us who would see the world more fully for what it is and learn to exist in that world as one who belongs—as one who strives to be in right relationship with the very many people with whom we share this world.

This work unfolds something deep and beautiful within you as a result, though. Life slowly becomes filled with experiences that validate your efforts, showing you just how much more there is to the world, how very full and alive it is. And those experiences— those moments when you have an unexpected but incredibly honest interaction with a spirit—make it difficult to go back to your old views and ways of being. They leave you craving more and make it so you won't want to see the world for anything less than what you now know it to be.

What Is a Spirit?

As a term, spirit refers to a spectrum of beings that exist primarily in energetic form. Some of these beings once possessed physical form, such as the spirits of dead humans and dead animals. Some of these beings currently possess or are bound to physical form, such as the spirits of plants, stones, mountains, rivers, forests, meadows, and arroyos. Some of these beings have never possessed physical form, neither will they physically incarnate in the future. Some of these beings exist bound to natural objects, some of them exist within man-made objects.

Those spirits who are bound to a physical form are not able to leave that physical form. This means that the only way that you can encounter these specific spirits is by being in proximity to them— that is, you must be physically near to their physical form in order to interact with them in any way. You cannot be miles away and communicate with them through divination, not even with the use of a nature-themed Tarot deck or an altar erected to the spirit beforehand. Those actions are as effective for communicating with these types of spirits (such as the spirit of a tree or river) as they would be for having a conversation with your closest friend.

Many spirits do not have physical form yet they remain within a general area, moving freely about the physical world as they please. These spirits, too, cannot be communicated with without proximity; there are no actions that you can—or should—take at home that will change that. Generally, most spirits want absolutely nothing to do with us. They are not interested in us and they do not want to interact with us. They may even respond in a hostile manner if their right to consent—the consent to the interaction—is disregarded. There is a reason why so many folk tales, from cultures across the planet, depict land spirits as some of the most dangerous spirits that can be encountered.

Spirits owe us nothing.

The fact that we are witches does not mean that the spirit world is waiting around for us to reach out and say "hi," or for us to make an offering so they can bestow upon us gifts, knowledge, and healing. Although common, these ideas are directly at odds with animism as they prioritize living human desires and existence over that of any spirit. This creates a hierarchy that places living humans in a position of power, importance, and value over all other beings. You can look around and see how well that attitude is working for us, creating a society that is terrified of intimacy and views other living humans as resources that either provide a benefit in some way or should be thrown away and replaced with a newer, shinier human that holds more benefit to us personally.

Yet animism tells us that all beings have intrinsic value that cannot be taken away. All beings are important and to be respected. In working to adopt the worldview of animism, you will frequently encounter the need to decenter yourself, your perspective, your opinions, and even your experiences. You will be reminded, repeatedly, that your perspective, your opinions, and your experiences are not universal—among humans or among spirits.

However, this is typically one of the most challenging aspects of animism to accept. It is an idea that we find ourselves butting our heads against over and over, as we slowly peel back the layers of non-animistic worldviews and find ourselves once again needing to unpack the full context of what it means to decenter humans. Ideas that we are special can help us to get through challenging situations, help us to endure trauma and abuse that we don't deserve but are unable to stop in that moment. The value of such ideas in those moments is not to be dismissed, yet they are a reaction to a worldview that says that individuality, autonomy, and personhood are directly tied to concepts of power—and that power exists only in relation to others (power over or under) and that power must be fought for in terms of acquirement and retention.

Animism rejects the worldview that creates and sustains such abuse, and it can provide us a pathway that supports our efforts to heal from such past instances of abuse—we may not be special but neither are we beneath anyone else. In prizing all beings and rejecting hierarchies, animism operates from the default position that power over others cannot be sought because it does not exist to be had in the first place. Instead, animism emphasizes the connection shared among us and presents us with obligation to ensure that we are in right relationship with each other, including that we are in right relationship with ourselves. This, in turn, asks us to consider if we are doing what we can to ensure our actions are not causing harm or distress and that they are supporting each being's right to have their needs met and cared for. In respecting the individuality and autonomy of every being—regardless of whether that being is living human, plant, animal, human dead, or other noncorporeal spirit—we decenter ourselves and learn to see the world in a way that places us as one among many, not better than but a part of, and that's a transformative place in which to find ourselves.

Later in this lesson, we'll discuss the general types of spirits that you could encounter in your local area. For now, it is enough for us to note that the physical world is quite literally full of spirits. It is unusual (though not uncommon) to come upon an area—be it outside or some sort of building—that is empty of spirits. These locations are known as dead zones and are really obvious when you encounter them. There is an emptiness and sterility to them that can make it difficult to feel comfortable in these places. Generally, dead zones are the result of trauma within that place, such as a forest that has been recently clear cut—quite literally removing a significant number of spirits from that forest—or when a house has been heavily remodeled. (Note that newly built houses will have a similar feel to them, due to the absence of spirits, but spirits will begin naturally arriving to and existing within the home as a consequence to humans living there. This demonstrates a clear relationship between human domesticity and the presence of certain types of spirits within human dwellings—such as brownies, domoviye, or those unnamed spirits that like to linger in doorways, peeking around the corner to watch their human housemates.) These places will heal independently, however, it is possible to facilitate that healing, such as through reforestation, removing garbage, and otherwise interacting with that place in a compassionate way.

While many spirits exist without physical form, it is important to note that spirits and energy are not the same thing. As we noted in Lesson 1: Witchcraft and Worldview, we don't know what energy is. Rather, it's a term that we use—however imperfectly—to speak of spiritual forces and the substance of which spirits are comprised (regardless if they have physical form). While experiences show us that the something that is there (and that we call energy) exists, those same experiences show us that although spirits are comprised of energy, energy does also exist distinct from spirits.

Energy healing is common among witches, and involves projecting energy (as you did in Exercise 1: Push and Pull in the previous lesson) from yourself and into someone else's body. This is not you putting your spirit into that person, just energy. Likewise, it is possible to remove your spirit body from your physical body to travel to the Otherworld (as you'll do in Lesson 6: The Layered World), yet there will still be energy within your physical body. Another example demonstrating this clear difference between energy and spirits is that you can cut a leaf from a plant and both that plant and that leaf will contain energy, but only the plant will contain a spirit. Similarly, you can trim your nails or your hair and your spirit will remain within your physical body. It will not be wholly contained in each nail clipping or snipped strand of hair.

Energy also exists in great flowing currents, moving through the cosmos much like the wind, carrying influences as well as influencing in its own right. And still there are smaller currents of energy moving about us: energy that is the consequences of actions and choices, energy that is the rippling of emotions, and even the energy sent forth with the casting of a spell. That energy doesn't return to you and it doesn't even necessarily originate from within you as energy can be raised—pulled from some sort of source or even created—to be used for a spell, as well as be generated through physical actions with no connection to magickal action (such as through physical exercise or even brushing your hair).

Personhood of Spirits

In all things there is a spirit, and each of those spirits is unique, individual, and autonomous. They are not a part of some larger whole, rather, they are each distinct. And each spirit possesses personhood and are to be understood as *people*. That we are able to interact with these spirits—both through spiritual techniques like divination and direct communication, which uses skills founded in the awareness of spiritual forces and spiritual beings—supports their personhood and underscores the obligation we have as animists to be in right relationship with these spirits, with these people.

Concepts of personhood—and to whom it is and is not granted—do differ among the animist worldviews of many Indigenous peoples. The animism that we are covering throughout this book does not come from any particular Indigenous tradition nor through the study of any Indigenous traditions. This animism is based on my lived experience as someone who was taught witchcraft by the spirits of the land and has spent a lifetime in rural and remote places, and it heavily reflects the opinions of spirits that are typically found in areas not dominated by human presence. And these spirits say they are all people. They all possess personhood. Considering that many land spirits are ancient, powerful, and honestly some of the most dangerous spirits we could ever encounter, I'm not one to question their words.

This concept, that all spirits have personhood and are people, is where we begin to see animism exerting its influence and affecting our behavior. Because if all spirits are people, and all things contain a spirit, then living humans are not unique. We exist as one type of person in a world filled with people. We are one among many.

There is no value-based difference among these people. Humans are not better than any non-human person. Living humans are not better than dead humans. There are, rather, many different types of people existing together, sharing space together. And humans happen to be just one type of person.

Seeing this personhood and acknowledging it through your actions is how animism is lived because, without separation among these various types of people, the relationships among them become more prominent. And so, how we interact with them is important to consider. Are we acting in ways that show the spirits around us respect? Are we acting in ways that acknowledge their right of existence?

Animism as a lived worldview demands that you live in right relationship with all people, to the best of your ability. Right relationship is the actions you take that are congruent with the awareness of the relationship that exists between you and another being and the awareness of inarguable autonomy of each being. It is acting in such a way so as to minimize negative impact upon the beings closest to you. It is acting in such a way so as to encourage and work toward mutual benefit for all, as much as is possible. This effort to be in right relationship with the world around us, as best as you can, is animism in action. This is how it is lived.

When first adopting an animist worldview, it can be difficult to be mindful of the spirits around you. After all, how can you be sure they exist? Materialist worldviews that prioritize humans as the only type of persons and that disconnect us from an objectified land encourage the dismissal of the potential existence of spirits. Yet materialism cannot explain nor prove consciousness, something with which you have daily experience. If we cannot prove that our consciousness exists then we can, similarly, not disapprove nor discount—without great hubris—the existence of consciousness in other physical beings—not just animals but also plant life and those things that we term inanimate, such as rocks, mountains, and rivers. Animism encourages us to avoid such hubris.

From there, it can be difficult to conceive of these spirits as truly autonomous and alive. The influence of Victorian era scientific naturalism remains strong in Euro-American society, with concepts such as ecosystems—where every plant, animal, insect, and the like, exists as a cog in a machine, performing a mechanical function that keeps the ecosystem machine running smoothly and productively. This mechanical view of nature also contributes to the one-to-one translation of correspondences that is so prevalent within the witchcraft community, which disregards the existence of the spirit within that object (never mind their personhood) and how a relationship with that spirit can override and negate even the most frequently shared correspondence.

Understanding Your Local Spirits

As witches, we often talk about looking for the wiggle room in regard to spellcraft—these are the areas where we are able to influence things, where changes can be made. In all things, you have the ability to influence things most closely related to and in proximity to yourself. For example, you can most easily influence changes first in your thoughts, then in your actions, then in the people with whom you live, and then expanding further to include your community, the city in which you live, and on and outward. While you can most strongly influence the people you live and work with, there is greater difficulty in directly influencing random people that live in the same city as you.

In regard to living as a witch, living as someone in awareness of the many spirit people that fill the world, local spirits encompass all spirits who are in closest proximity to you: those spirits with whom you most frequently come into contact and those spirits with whom you are most likely to come into contact. Local spirits are those spirits who are most easily, strongly affected by the choices you make.

With that in mind, there are three general types of spirits, based on location, that make up local spirits. These are not the only types of spirits that exist or that you might even reasonably expect to encounter within your witchcraft practice (as these are, admittedly, very broad categories). But these are types of spirits that are absolutely around you right now and with whom you can begin focusing on being in right relationship right now.

- land spirits

- house and building spirits

- the spirits of man-made objects

Land Spirits

Land spirits is a broad term that refers to spirits who are bound to natural physical objects, animate and inanimate, as well as the spirits of natural processes. It includes the spirits of plants, trees, and the wind, but it also includes spirits of locations, such as the spirit of a forest that exists separate from the spirit within each and every tree and plant within that forest, separate from each and every animal within that forest, separate from each and every spirit without physical form that calls that forest home. These spirits of locations (such as our forest spirit example, or the spirit of a lake, a sea, or a field) are just as unique as any type of spirit can be. The spirit of a forest on one side of your hometown is not the same spirit of another forest on the other side of town. They are different people and they have different personalities, interests, and predispositions—and they may behave in entirely different ways toward you, should they choose to acknowledge you at all.

Land spirits can also include the spirits of dead humans and dead animals that have not crossed over. With dead animals, these spirits typically become guardian spirits of a place, with their appearance altering dramatically as time passes. They may appear to have plants and fungi growing upon them or even to be made of minerals. Dead humans, on the other hand, typically become parasitic and may seek to harm you in some way, should you encounter them. Their appearance typically changes as time passes, too, rendering them something vaguely human looking. Remember, there is a reason why folklore is filled with stories of land spirits consuming and otherwise murdering living humans. Spirits do not exist for the witch or for living humans. They are their own people, with their own lives, interests, and motives. Many land spirits—such as trolls, shimmers, or the parasitic human dead example above—are absolutely to be avoided and protected against should you be planning to venture into their domains. As much as you may seek to establish yourself as someone who belongs to the land, rooting yourself to a particular location and doing the work to be respectful and build relationships with the spirits who call that location home, know that it is impossible to have a personal relationship with every local to you land spirit. There are simply too many. Every plant, every stone, every natural feature, every clearing, every dense forest, the wind, the clouds, it cannot be done. But you can still take care to be in right relationship with these spirits. And that effort—those relationships you tend and friends that you make—will have a significant effect on you as a witch.

House and Building Spirits

House and building spirits are the spirits of and within buildings. Much like a forest, each building has a spirit who isn't so much bound to that entire physical structure as they are that structure, and then that physical structure also contains many smaller spirits who live within it. A house is very similar to the human physical body, in that there is the spirit of that house (you) and then so many spirits who live within it and affect the overall well-being of that house (your gut flora and fauna, the cute little mites on your eyelashes, the bacteria across your skin, and the like). In this way, there is a vibrant community of spirits that exists with any building—all of whom exist separate from each other and yet affect each other, influencing the atmosphere of that building. The building simultaneously exists separate from all its inhabitants, a thinking, feeling being in its own right.

Similar to natural locations (like forests or lakes), there are some generalities that can be made in regard to the types of spirits that can be found in specific types of buildings. For example, there are certain types of spirits who live within homes but who do not live within office buildings, coffee shops, or barns. There are some spirits who can only be found in doorways, while others can only be found in windows; some who prefer to peek around corners and watch as you go about your day, others who will hide in the darkest corners of the home and yell at you when you intrude upon their space. And still there are other types of spirits who do not generally have any associations with buildings of any type yet will wander inside (for whatever reason), decide they like it there, and take up residency.

There does not appear to be any limitation on type of building and whether it contains spirits, although newer buildings will generally possess fewer spirits (some need time to find their way inside, some may be overwhelmed by their existence—much like a newborn baby—and require time to adjust and become more strongly evident) and buildings that experience high amounts of traffic from living humans (such as public buildings, like large stores, or apartment buildings) tend to also have a greater number of transient spirits—spirits who pass through these buildings but rarely stick around for very long. House and building spirits are very accessible spirits to begin interacting with and are a beautiful example of how statements of there being no spirits in places where humans have significantly altered the landscape (that is, cities, suburban areas, industrial zones, and the like) are patently false—humans are not so special or so powerful as to be able to exert that kind of power.

Spirits of Man-Made Objects

The spirits of man-made objects are frequently the single most difficult type of spirit to begin interacting with, never mind to accept the existence of, despite it being the type of spirit with whom we have the most familiarity and with whom we spend the most time. It is here the worldview of animism clashes most heavily with that of the overculture, making clear how radically different the two worldviews are and how unsupportive our society is to living as a witch and animist. Yet, if there exists a spirit within a rock, within a piece of quartz, within a house made of wood, concrete, and wall to wall carpeting, it is not such a great leap to recognize the spirit within any man-made object.

Yet it is frequently touted, in magickal circles, that man-made objects are inferior to natural objects, that they contaminate a magickal space, that they hold no innate energy, that they are a void. These ideas are a great example of destructive attitudes finding their way into witchcraft. Due to a lack of examination or consideration of how these ideas stand up against basic values and worldviews, they become additional baggage that we need to work through as part of our efforts to grow as people and sink ourselves deeper into the waters of animism and witchcraft.

With that in mind, we can see how these ideas are rooted in widespread belief that all objects are disposable. We can also see how they are founded in the pain we hold from living in a society that actively works to keep us divorced from the natural world— not just through ideas like human supremacy but through reinforcement of ideas such as that the natural world is a resource or that our own purpose is to labor and be productive (to also exist as a resource). Add to this the encouragement to objectify the land (commonly taking the form of romanticism among witches), that serves to bolster that separation and rid us of any sense of accountability to the land, and it's no surprise that man-made objects might be viewed so derisively.

There is nothing that we are capable of making that is not produced from or comprised of materials natural to this world. That humans placed their hands upon them, altered their shape, and gave them a new and different form does not make these objects less important than natural objects. We are not so powerful—be it because we're "amazing" or "terrible"—to be capable of exerting that kind of force upon physical materials. Consider how long plastic items remain in existence, stubbornly defying the process of decay. How is this spirit less important than the spirit within a piece of sandstone slowly being worn away by wind and rain? There is no difference. Shape and form do not change the value of a person.

Exercises

While reading about important concepts and techniques can do a lot to expand your awareness of what is possible and even give you benchmarks for your practice, nothing compares with what you learn through direct experiences. Through taking action—doing witchcraft—you take the knowledge you've acquired and transform it into wisdom, seating it bone deep within you and making it something that is usable and supports your practice.

In witchcraft, it is all about the doing and not the collecting of information. And so, this lesson holds three exercises for you to continue building upon what you've read with personal experience that shows you, firsthand, the truth behind those words and why we are approaching things this way. The first exercise should take no more than ten minutes to complete, though you may wish to repeat it over the course of a few days in order to better develop skill. The second exercise should take about twenty to thirty minutes, less if you have experience with energy work (maybe five to ten minutes). The third exercise is potentially more intensive in preparation, depending on where you live and your limitations. However, the actual doing of the third exercise should take no more than an hour.

Exercise 1: Practicing Discernment—Energy Exercise

One of the most critical skills you can develop as a witch that will help you to take your practice deeper and further is discernment. We noted that discernment has two meanings in witchcraft, for this exercise it is discernment as the skill of telling *this* from *that* to which we are referring. This skill is what allows you to tell the difference between energy currents and spirit presence, between spirit communication and your imagination. It's also what helps you to tell one spirit from another and to recognize spirit presences as specific spirits that you have interacted with before (which can be quite useful as you won't necessarily always "see" a spirit that is near to you). Discernment is the skill that brings precision and accuracy to what you are sensing so that you can more accurately identify and understand what's going on, helping you to potentially respond more effectively.

For this exercise, you're going to feel the energy of similar objects in order to ascertain any differences between them.

The following objects are suggestions, you can try this exercise with all or some of them:

- a live plant and dried herbs

- potting soil and soil from outside

- a fresh vegetable and the same type of vegetable cooked

Use the same actions as you did in Exercise 2: Scavenger Hunt of Lesson 1: Witchcraft and Worldview, slowly turning your attention to the object, opening your awareness to it, and taking care to only feel the energy within the object and to not push your energy into it. If you found the Centering Exercise helpful or are still working on consistently feeling energy, you may wish to center beforehand.

You may wish to record your observations, noting what you felt for each object and then noting the similarities and differences between each object and its counterpart.

Exercise 2: Grounding—Energy Exercise

While some of the basic movements of this exercise may be familiar to you if you have prior experience in energy work, it's important to note that the details (and any differences to what you've previously done) are fundamental to its mechanics. Just as altering the mechanics of a motion with your physical body will yield different results (for example, lifting something heavy with your back muscles versus using your leg muscles), altering the details of this exercise will yield different results—the proof of which you are able to confirm with your discernment skills.

At the most basic level, this is a grounding exercise: it reorients you within the world around you by creating a complete energetic circuit between you and the Earth and between you and the cosmos. This is similar to an electrical circuit in that multiple pathways are required to get the desired result but that's really as far as this analogy goes.

What the energetic circuit you're creating does, rather, is establish a purposeful connection between you (an energy generating and containing source) with two very large energy generating and containing sources (with whom you already share an intimate connection by virtue of your existence). And as a result of that connection, a current of moving energy is created through you. That flow of energy has a stabilizing (for lack of a better word) effect on your energy and spirit body, helping you to be better oriented with your energetic surroundings.

This can be an effective preparatory exercise for spirit communication, energy healing, other energy exercises, spellcraft, or journeying. It can also be a very helpful exercise to include in your aftercare for more intense acts of magick that leave you feeling out of sorts, nauseated, or weak.

As you'll see throughout this book, this exercise can be easily adapted to achieve different results. Our focus with the steps as written here, is to have a grounding effect, practice feeling and moving energy, and stretch your awareness skills.

Please remember that deliberately altering the pattern of your breathing can aggravate physical health concerns and may pose a substantial risk to your health and safety. In the instances where this risk is minimal, you may comfortably work within your limitations by altering your environment—such as by ensuring you are surrounded by pillows in case you pass out; in instances where the risks outweigh the benefits of practicing moving energy with breath, modify the exercise as is necessary for your safety. Breath work can be eliminated from this exercise, with extra emphasis placed on visualization, as an option.

Sit or lie down so that your spine is as straight as possible but you're still comfortable (sitting may be easier the first few times you do this exercise, due to the imagery and movements). Close your eyes and take a deep breath, consciously relaxing your body as much as you're able. Take a moment to center yourself: slowing your breathing so that your inhalations and exhalations are even. Focus on your breathing until you notice your physical body relaxing more.

Now, inhale. As you do so, pull energy from the Earth below you up and into your body, focusing on it entering through your pelvic floor, moving upward through your body, and resting at about your midsection. It can be helpful to visualize the energy not so much filling the lower half of your body but being contained within a hollow channel that runs vertically through the center of your body, from your pelvic floor to the crown of your head (to where the anterior fontanelle was when you were a baby).

Exhale, focusing on holding that energy at your midsection. Inhale again and pull more energy up and into your channel, where it joins the energy you previously pulled into you. Exhale, holding the energy there.

This time as you inhale, pull energy up from the Earth and into your channel through your pelvic floor again but keep the energy moving up and through your midsection, following your channel upward. As you exhale, push the energy out through the top of your channel. Visualize and feel the energy leave you.

Repeat this movement—pulling energy from the Earth up through the bottom of your channel, moving it through your channel, and sending it out through the top of your channel—until it is comfortable to maintain.

Now you will repeat the basic movements, but reversed: pull energy from the cosmos down into your channel (through the top of your head), hold it at your midsection, and then move it out through the bottom of your channel (through your pelvic floor). Repeat for however many times you moved the energy up through your channel (if you pulled energy up and through your channel four times, then pull energy down and out your channel for four repetitions).

This is where things may get trickier . . .

Now you're going to perform both movements at the same time: inhale and pull energy up and into your channel while you simultaneously pull energy down and into your channel, holding the energy at your midsection. Inhale and pull more energy into you.

As you exhale, continue the movements of energy through your midsection, focusing on the energy from below and the energy from above twining about each other as they continue their course upward or downward through your channel.

Inhale and repeat the combined action again, focusing on the energy twining about each other, much like DNA, and passing into and out of your channel. Repeat the action for however many times you need to until it is comfortable to maintain.

Pay attention to any sensations you experience. There may be physical sensations that accompany the actions of this exercise:

you may feel the muscles of your pelvic floor contract or relax, you may feel yourself shift and sit up taller, you may feel your posture pull inward. There may be spiritual sensations: you may feel more expansive at times, you may feel more constricted and contained at other moments, you may feel more aware. Make a note of what you felt and at what point in the exercise you felt such.

Outline of Steps, Part 1

1. Sit comfortably. Close your eyes and center.

2. Inhale and pull energy up from the Earth and into your body, focusing on it entering through your pelvic floor, moving upward through a hollow channel, and resting at about your midsection. Exhale.

3. Inhale and pull more energy up and in through the bottom of your channel and moving through your midsection. Exhale and focus on sending the energy up through your channel and out of you through the top of your head.

4. Repeat multiple times, until the movement is comfortable to maintain.

Outline of Steps, Part 2

1. Inhale and pull energy down from the cosmos and into your body, focusing on it entering through the top of your head, moving downward through a hollow channel, and resting at about your midsection. Exhale.

2. Inhale and pull more energy down and in through the top of your channel and moving through your midsection. Exhale and focus on sending the energy down through your channel and out through your pelvic floor.

3. Repeat multiple times, until the movement is comfortable to maintain.

Outline of Steps, Part 3

1. As you inhale, simultaneously pull energy up into your channel and down into your channel. Exhale and allow the energy to rest at your midsection. Inhale and pull energy up into you and down into you again, this time breath the energy through your midsection, focusing on the energy twining about each other as the upward moving energy continues its course upward and the downward moving energy continues its course down.

2. Exhale and push the energy out through the top of your head and out through your pelvic floor.

3. Repeat multiple times, until the action is comfortable.

4. Record any sensations and observations in your notes.

Exercise 3: To Be Aware

This exercise is one of discovery but primarily awareness practiced in a controlled way. You will need to go outside, preferably somewhere with a fair amount of plant life, where there are minimal (or no) living humans present, and where you feel comfortable and safe letting your guard down a bit in order to have an experience. This could be your backyard, it could be a local park or nature preserve; it could be an abandoned lot that the land is slowly reclaiming and has a strong touch of alterity about it. It should be someplace that you can visit again easily, as you will need to return to this location in subsequent lessons as part of practicing new skills and working to deepen your relationship with this place and the many spirits who call it home. For this exercise, you will be opening your awareness to the presence of spirits.

Wherever it is that you go for this exercise, make sure that it is somewhere you are truly safe to not be wholly focused on your surroundings—be it because of wild animals or the dangers of other living humans. The fact that you will be there to do a spiritual exercise will not keep you safe from harm. Common sense does not go out the window because it's witchcraft.

Pause at the edge of the place where you will be completing this exercise. Close your eyes and focus on opening up your awareness to what is there to be sensed around you. This is a receptive state, where you allow yourself to see what is there to be seen, to hear what is there to be heard. This is not a state of seeking; it is passive and open.

When you activate your awareness, you see the world differently. Your focus is softer and details become fuzzier. It is easier to see energetic traces and movements. If there are other people with whom you do this exercise, you may very well notice a physical change in each other's expressions. The eyes will be half-closed, the muscles of the face relaxed.

To activate your awareness is to enter an altered state of consciousness, where you let slip your hold on the physical world to better perceive the spirit world about you. It is a light trance, but it is very easy to achieve, as you will discover. Just close your eyes, take a deep breath, focus on how you are making that shift to be more aware, exhale, and open your eyes.

Now, step into that place. Walk about the land taking note of what you see and feel. Go with no intention but to be open to having an experience. Hold an open awareness of your surroundings, a noticing without giving an overt indication of noticing, acknowledging without intention. It is a taking note of "yep, that's a thing." It's a manner of expressing receptivity without expectation. Expectation is your downfall. The spirits owe you nothing.

Take care that you do not push your energy outward and that you are focused only on being aware and sensing what may or may not be there. This is not an exercise of seeking or finding, this is an exercise of awareness: of simply experiencing what is there to be experienced.

Afterward, record your observations and any sensations you had. Remember to note things that you felt physically, such as a tightening in your core or a tingling on the back of your skull, but also note the way that your thoughts and emotions changed as you moved around and were near to different objects.

This exercise can be done during the day or at night; you may wish to experiment with repeating the exercise during different times to compare and contrast results.

Ongoing Exercises

- Continue to practice feeling the energy of objects and living beings from Lesson 1. Remember to focus on feeling the energy of that object or being and not to focus on sensing the spirit within it. Also remember how casual this can be, with you taking a moment to feel an object as you interact with and go about your day.

- Revisit your list of obstacles and opportunities from Lesson 2. Do any of the obstacles seem different now, as you learn and experience more? Is there anything you might remove from the list? Anything you might add? Perhaps there is more nuance and greater insight that you can add to some of the obstacles you noted that helps with working through them.

- Continue to work on identifying three to five local plants and three to five local trees, and finding out as much information about them as you can. While this doesn't replace direct interaction with these plants and trees, it is a good way to become more aware of your neighbors and the land upon which you live.

Final Note

Through awareness and action, animism takes hold of you, helping you to live your life in a way that decenters yourself and relieves the pressure that can come with perceiving the type of existence you hold (or "should" hold) as being of greater value than others. Instead of working to prove your worth—pushing yourself to achieve more, to achieve perfection, to always be striving and fighting—animism says that you are inherently valuable, worthy of respect, and deserving of love and care, just as all beings are regardless of their shape or form.

In many ways, adopting an animist worldview can be a radical act, as there is a vulnerability that comes with choosing to care about yourself and others. Yet through that caring you can find true connection and reinstill within yourself a feeling of purpose and belonging—both to the land as well as with the many beings (human and non-human) with whom you share the land.

Lesson 4

Being in Community

One of the great harms that individualist Western society has committed is that of convincing us we are alone in the world. Where a sense of belonging and safety once thrived now lies fear, encouraging us to act in desperation and mistrust of each other. We have forgotten how to have healthy relationships with each other, viewing other people through the lens of how they benefit us or how much they stand in between us and what we want. And so, it is of little surprise that most of us grow up with no understanding of what healthy community looks like, with no understanding that the desperation that drives us is due to the lack of connection we have to others.

We are not meant to be alone.

As much as it can be difficult to adjust behavior to account for the existence of so many spirit people in the world, it is developing an understanding of what it means to be in community—and subsequently learning to foster those relationships that is typically the greatest obstacle in adopting an animist worldview. There are dangers in trusting, there is heartache to be found in trying, and there are endless lessons in the importance of boundaries and obligations. It is difficult work, and yet learning to be in community with each other—learning to give a damn about each other—is the basic requirement of animism. It is the single greatest trait that distinguishes this worldview, both in general as well as in our behavior as animists. And it is the single greatest hope for the future that animism so freely offers us.

Relationships Mean Community

We've noted that animism is more than belief but a way of life. That way of life—the ways in which we act and interact with the world, including with beings corporeal and noncorporeal, animate and inanimate—comes down to a single two-fold point: awareness and acknowledgment of the relationships that naturally exist between us and all other beings. That acknowledgment is important because, without it, there arise inconsistencies between claimed belief and values and that of actions. Our actions reveal our beliefs and values as much as they do our hopes and our priorities. This isn't just a matter of repeated action solidifying those things within us. It's the way those things hold so tightly to us that we can't help but act in ways that reflect them. Those things that we hold most dear, the beliefs and values that drive us, can't help but be revealed through the way we move through the world. This is why multiple Pagan religious traditions have maxims along the lines of "you are known by your actions" and why animism can only be lived and not practiced.

Our society tends to view a relationship as a connection between two parties that is known and maintained by both parties through their interaction. From an animist (and specifically within the context of witchcraft) perspective, the definition of relationship is a bit broader, viewing it as the interplay between two parties—including energetic interplay. For example, imagine two people who have never met, never interacted, and have no idea of the other's existence. Through our society's lens, these people would be viewed as not having a relationship. But through an animist lens, a relationship does exist between them.

The animist understanding of relationship is dependent upon the accepted existence of a connection between one being and every other being. It is incredibly similar to the concept of interconnection often discussed within Paganism. This connection, this relationship, is innate to existence and cannot be removed. This connection between you and all other beings in our world—be they human, animal, plant, mineral, force of nature, or purely energetic—is fundamental to animism.

> In this way, a relationship exists between two parties regardless of proximity and regardless of knowledge of each other. To put that another way, our actions are able to affect others without our awareness of them, without our intention to impact them, and without our knowledge of that impact.
>
> Right relationship is the actions we take that are congruent with the awareness of a relationship and the inarguable autonomy of both parties. In this way, right relationship is the result of the choices we make so that our actions and existence do

not adversely affect someone else—regardless if they are living human or spirit being.

If a relationship is the inherent connection that exists between us and all other beings within the world, right relationship is the actions we take that are congruent with the awareness of that relationship and the awareness of inarguable autonomy of each being. It is acting in such a way so as to minimize negative impact upon the beings closest to us, and to encourage and work toward mutual benefit for all, as much as is possible.

So, as witches, when we speak of being in right relationship with our local spirits—the spirits with whom we share our homes, the spirits we encounter outside of our homes, the spirits within the objects upon which we depend for a happy, healthy life—we are talking about not being assholes to these spirits. Instead, we are talking about identifying and acting in ways that afford these spirits similar respect as that which we extend to living humans and non-human beings.

This is absolutely part of what is meant by saying that witchcraft is work. It's not a path that is supported by our society; it is the antithesis to the worldview of our society and hegemonic overculture. Making an effort to live in right relationship with the spirits around us can alienate us from the living humans nearest to us because they don't understand. They have no precedent to which they can compare our actions, and so the idea itself, that our actions could adversely impact a rock in the yard and such action should be avoided (for example), meets a brick wall in their minds. But we can hope that our actions set an example. We can strive to be in right relationship with those around us, regardless of their personal worldview, and hope that the respect and awareness we demonstrate ripple outward.

To Be in Right Relationship

The awareness of the potential larger ripples of our actions is part of the concept of being in right relationship. Those with whom we are in right relationship are connected to others with whom they are in (right) relationship. And where multiple relationships exist—where multiple people are connected and affecting each other—community exists.

As we noted in Lesson 2: Witchcraft Comes from the Land,

"To sink ourselves more deeply into animism is to sink
ourselves more deeply into the web of relationships and
the web of community, binding ourselves to those around
us through mutual awareness, respect, and obligation."

It is obligation that binds community and that allows for the existence of trust and a sense of safety between you and someone with whom you are in community. The act of being in mutually understood right relationship requires everyone to make choices with the well-being of everyone in mind. In this way, the actions we take depend upon what we can identify as the most likely outcome for those around us. For example, you and a friend have gotten into an argument. They said something that really hurt you, but they apologized and you forgave them. Later, you bring up that they had said something hurtful in conversation with someone else, dismissing the fact that they had apologized and you forgave them. There's no point in bringing up the argument except to make them look bad to this other person and encourage them to not trust your friend. In doing so, you betray the mutually understood trust between the two of you and demonstrate that you cannot be fully trusted to this other person. Your actions show that you are not in right relationship with either party.

Community means everyone—including us. Animism does not ask us to prize others over ourselves but, rather, asks us to prize everyone equally. Just as much as we must strive to be in right relationship with those closest to us, we must strive to be in right relationship with ourselves. This can present unique obstacles depending on personal background. For example, our society typically teaches white people to center themselves and that they, personally, are exceptional. Yet Black, Indigenous, and other people of color typically have it impressed upon them that their worth is secondary to others. Both situations—while different yet intrinsic to white supremacy as a systemic force—demonstrate a distorted view of the self in relation to others, affecting one's ability to be in right relationship with others (how can you be in right relationship with someone when you're acting within a hierarchical power dynamic in that relationship?) and affect one's ability to be in right relationship with yourself (how can you be in right relationship with yourself with a weak sense of self?).

Likewise, while community does mean everyone, someone who actively and consciously abuses others demonstrates, through their actions, that they do not agree to the obligations of being in community. Prizing community does not mean to give countless opportunities to someone to abuse others, nor does it mean refusing to erect and maintain boundaries to safeguard ourselves and others. You cannot strive to ensure your efforts do not cause direct harm without likewise taking effort to protect against other forms of harm, as much as is possible.

Being in Right Relationship with the Land

Many of us don't know how to have healthy relationships with the Land because we don't know how to have healthy relationships with other living humans. This underscores why the idea of community can be both intoxicating and terrifying, and why there are so many obstacles between us and achieving it.

Too often, when coming to spirit work, we repeat the patterns of relationships with which we're most familiar with the spirits we are attempting to befriend. This highlights why it is so crucial for us to unpack our baggage and confront unconscious bias because these are the patterns that we will replicate in our relationships with the land and its spirits.

This baggage can be the result of influence from:

· the overculture, such as its ideas of being "stewards" (that is, ones who manage from a position of power over) of the Earth

· religious baggage from previously held religions or religious hegemony (such as that belief and intention matter more than actions, regardless of the impact of one's actions or lack of action)

This baggage can also result from within the witchcraft community, such as through the influence of the New Age and New

Thought movements that has seeped so fully into witchcraft as to be indistinguishable to those who are just starting out. We see this particular influence demonstrated through a general attempt to spiritualize aspects of Euro-American culture that provide personal benefit while affording an absence of accountability, such as exploitation of minoritized religions and cultures via appropriation or the banner of "universalism," ableism presented as scientific skepticism (such as through conspiracies surrounding vaccines and medications), or law of attraction and manifestation in regards to physical and mental health (such as statements that good physical and mental health can be achieved through thoughts alone, blaming the individual for illness or disability and thus justifying lack of accommodations or concern for them), or toxic positivity that refuses acknowledgment of anything that could result in personal discomfort.

While these examples, in particular, can seem relevant to social issues alone, they impact the relationships we are capable of having with the land and its spirits due to how that perspective, as an initial worldview, impacts our actions. That perspective encourages us to center our wants and our comfort over consideration for how our actions impact the world, and people, around us—as well as consideration of the ways small changes to our actions can positively impact the world, and people, around us in exchange for slight discomfort on our parts. For example, you might spend a weekend removing invasive plant species from a plot of land because the result of the blisters on your hands is the continued presence of native plants and pollinators in that area, as well as the local land spirits witnessing your concern for these members of your community and thus being more agreeable to your presence and requests

Alive with Spirits

for interaction. Unpacking this baggage and doing the hard work to deconstruct and understand where you encounter resistance to adopting a new worldview is essential in order to cultivate and maintain healthy relationships with the Land.

Relationships must be understood to be fluid and alive. Much like we approach witchcraft as a sentient creature, making demands of us and requiring appeasing, so too must we approach our relationship with the variety of spirits about us as alive, requiring tending, and obligating certain actions and behaviors from us. These actions define our efforts to be in right relationship with these spirits. And those efforts can lead to wonderful results, such as the development of relationships with specific spirits that are so strong and encompass so much trust that we can call that spirit an ally, knowing that they have our back and are there if we should need them.

Typically, relationships with your local spirits will have an ephemeral quality about them, as interactions with them can be fleeting, can be single events, or can happen in such a way that you're not sure if you are consistently interacting with one specific spirit or a group of similar spirits. Nonetheless, there are strong benefits to making an effort to be in right relationship with your local spirits.

- Doing so roots you more strongly to your physical location. This helps you to be someone who belongs in that local area rather than someone who is just there. Belonging is a quality extended by local spirits and cannot be claimed or assumed; it is only given. But its receipt greatly changes the experiences one has within that location as there is less friction between you and the local energy currents.

- Doing so roots you more strongly into witchcraft. In looking at the five traits of witchcraft (animism, divination, the Land, ritual, and spirit work) we see that being in right relationship with your local spirits hits three of those traits. That's a 60 percent increase of witchcraft in your life and a 60 percent increase in expanded skill, awareness, and potential capability to you as a witch.

- It opens you to the opportunity of new friends and allies. Taking action to be on good terms with your local spirits is the first step to building strong and mutually beneficial relationships with them. These relationships can grow, and those spirits may become treasured friends and even cherished allies—spirits who may help you in your witchcraft, working magick for you, boosting your spells, and generally having your back.

- It makes your life easier. While every relationship does not hold the potential to become a deep and personal relationship, making a point to be on good terms with the spirits around you increases the likelihood of them not viewing you as a nuisance and instead viewing you as a member of their community. That helps to minimize unwelcome surprises and challenges in your life that stem from external energetic sources—that is, be nice to your house spirits and they'll bounce a curse. They might even alert you to when your child wakes up from a nightmare but is too scared to call out to you in the night.

Getting to Know Your Local Spirits

There are some general things to keep in mind when introducing yourself to your local spirits. For example, remember that spirits owe you nothing. They don't owe you their attention, not even to tell you to go away. So even if you do everything right, show them the utmost respect and care, they may not want anything to do with you. And that's fine. That's their right. Spirits are allowed to say no.

In some cases, that spirit may want nothing to do with you because they just don't, the same way that we sometimes don't get along with another human regardless of their personality and quality of our interactions with them. In other cases, that spirit's decision could be based on their interactions with and observations of other humans. In many places throughout the world the physical land has been subjected to considerable exploitation—from colonialism throughout the so-called Americas to extractivism in the global south to individual humans behaving in destructive ways in specific locations. This has, understandably, given many spirits an unfavorable impression of living humans, with our general behavior showing that we are often best avoided. Yet mutually beneficial relationships with some of these spirits is still possible. And so, we try, because it matters and because it's one way that we can tug at the knot behind all these systems of harm and have some sort of effect, no matter how small.

Land Spirits

Keeping in mind that this is a broad term, it is impossible to have a personal relationship with every local-to-you land spirit. There are simply too many. But you can still take care to be in right relationship with these spirits.

- Be a guest, not an intruder. Anywhere you could ever be out in nature is home to numerous spirits. You can and will leave, going back to your home and attending to the basic means of your survival within that house/apartment/tiny traveling house/whatever. These spirits will not leave that place. It is their home. It is where they attend to the basic means of their survival. Remember your manners.

- Act in a way that minimizes harm, including taking action to reduce or repair the harm caused by others. This is absolutely me encouraging you to reduce your consumption and waste, to reuse the objects in your life until they can no longer be repaired and reused, to recycle, and to pick up trash everywhere outside. Be that person who has random bits of garbage in all their pockets; that's the real witchcraft aesthetic. Minimizing harm also means not treating the natural world as your own private metaphysical store. Ethical wildcrafting, or foraging, is possible and it starts with not seeing the natural world as a resource for you to exploit.

- Question your assumptions. There exists great benefit to us in being outside; it is crucial to our well-being as humans and essential for us as witches. As much as it does benefit us and is integral to our craft, we must remember that our society has largely extricated us from the natural world, encouraging us to live lives in opposition to a sense of oneness and belonging with nature and to view it as a resource from which we can take for our benefit. See it, want it, take it, have it, is the guiding thought of colonial, Euro-American society, and it is a difficult way of thinking from which to free ourselves. It makes it essential, when outside, to question things we may be likely to chalk up as spiritual experiences. For example, is that feather laying in the path before you truly a sign, is it yours to take or do you covet its beauty and feel it as deservingly yours? Is that plant calling out to you or do you feel its energy as it sharply asserts itself and tries to push you away? Are you "connecting with nature" or are you stomping about, leaking energy everywhere and pushing smaller spirits out of their homes, while soaking up all loose traces of energy because you can?

House Spirits

There are some things you can do that can be effective in helping you be in right relationship with the house and its spirits. First and foremost: care for your home. All the offerings, candles, and attempts to talk to your house spirits cannot achieve anything if your actions do not show that you care for the house—the being who provides you shelter and offers you solace.

- Keep your house clean. Yes, that means cleaning that nasty mess that's been beneath your kitchen sink, in your basement, behind your toilet for forever. Doesn't matter how yucky it is, clean it. Clean that pink mold out of your windowsills, too; wear a mask when you do.

- Appreciate the beauty of the house. As you clean your home, make a point of really seeing its beauty and uniqueness. See the way the colors of the molding blend together like honey and shine after you scrub off the built-up gunk. See how strong and solid the house is, the walls straight and free of cracks. See the way the afternoon sunlight pours in through the windows, bouncing off the floor, and making your house sing for the beauty of it. See the being of your house for who they are, find the beauty in them, praise that beauty.

- Keep your house in good condition. If something breaks, repair it quickly so that the damage is minimal. If what breaks isn't major enough to warrant a repair, do something to preserve the beauty of the house. One of the doors chips along the bottom? Cover the chip with paint so it matches the rest of the door and talk to the house as you do so, letting you know that you see the chip, that it's not serious, and that it doesn't change the house in your eyes.

- Be mindful of the spirit occupants. Hold back on cleansing your home down to a blank state. This can oust smaller house spirits for good and may dislocate larger spirits temporarily. Should you need to cleanse or purify your home, involve your house spirits, consulting them as to the how and letting them know why. They may very well suggest a particular method or specific herbs to burn (and herbs to absolutely not burn for the task).

- Avoid slamming doors. Be they entry doors, bedroom doors, or cupboard doors, avoid slamming or shutting these doors too loudly. The sound can be jarring to living and spirit occupants alike, and some cultures (such as the Hmong) say that there are small spirits that live in all doorways. Slamming those doors knocks them out of their homes. Remember, too, that all doorways are portals and, per our own witch lore, gatekeeper spirits are very much a thing and can be found in all such portals and doorways. Be mindful of these spirits.

Man-Made Objects

It can be more difficult to be aware of these spirits due to the incompatibilities between animism and that of the dominant Euro-American worldview. Also contributing to that difficulty is the fact that the spirits within newly created objects can be quite small and quiet. Like a newborn baby, they may be overwhelmed by their own existence and not know how to interact with others. They can be very preoccupied with just learning to be that you may not even be able to feel much of a presence. Your efforts will produce more noticeable results with older objects, however, this is not a reason to treat these spirits differently: someone's ability to benefit you is not a representation of their worth as a person (and these spirits absolutely possess personhood).

- Appreciate their beauty. Look at that object and truly see it. These spirits do not exist separate from their physical form; you cannot interact with them except through that physical form. So, see them, truly see them. Appreciate what makes them unique, what features define who they are. See the shapes and lines, see the colors and variation, see the texture. See what makes them who they are and the inherent beauty that form possesses.

- Appreciate their function. Man-made objects are generally made for a purpose. They have a function they are designed to fulfill. Of course, some of those objects fulfill that purpose more effectively than others, but this, too, is not an indicator of the worth of that spirit. See the purpose they are meant to fulfill, see the ways they fulfill it, the ways that they try. Appreciate those efforts and the ways the fulfillment of that purpose benefits you. See how the spirit of that object performing its function is a gift to you—a gift given and that can be taken away (how many times have you experienced an object suddenly breaking or becoming lost because you yelled at it?).

- Acknowledge their personhood through your actions. Talk to that object, sing it a happy song when you spend time together, praise it when it performs its function well, apologize if you drop it or bump into it accidentally, commiserate with it if it becomes broken and do what you can to repair or repurpose it. Treat that object like a friend and appreciate the time you share together. Some of the objects in your life spend more time with you than any living human will, some of the objects in your life will spend their entire existence in your care. How beautiful for them to grow old with you! How beautiful for those spirits to spend their entire lives with you! Do what you can to make sure that life is a good one.

Exercises

So much of what we do as witches builds upon the experiences we already have had. In this way, life experience that we've gained due to the unique circumstances that we've lived through—including our background and individual cultures—adds a layer of understanding that is subtly, yet potently, woven throughout our magick. Much like worldview, it informs what we do and how we do it.

It is the same with the foundational skills of witchcraft. You will continue to use the same basic skills throughout your practice, even should you practice for decades. But the manner in which those skills take shape changes; the ways in which you use those skills directly builds upon the experiences that you have as a witch. Every time you stretch your awareness to the world around you, holding in check your expectations, you open yourself to new experiences. Every time you flex your skills in energy work, feeling and directing energy without a second thought, you make possible your ability to perform other magickal actions as if they are second nature to you.

Everything you do as a witch now feeds the witch you are becoming, shaping your knowledge, strengthening your skills, and amplifying your capabilities. And so, for this lesson there are three new exercises for you to complete, each building off the work you've already done as part of working through this book and helping you to more fully see and live in the world as an animist.

Exercise 1: Contemplating Community— Journal Prompt

For this exercise you will be free writing on the concept of community and your experiences with community. There's no right or wrong way to approach this exercise as long as you are giving yourself time and space for your thoughts to wander. We've talked a lot about discernment as the skill of telling *this from that*: this is the other side of discernment. Discernment here is a contemplative practice where you allow your thoughts to wander, without judgment or expectations, so that insight can occur.

In this way, you are thinking about community (or another topic, you can use discernment as a contemplative practice for anything; it is strongly recommended to use it as such throughout your witchcraft practice) not for the purpose of solving a problem or even necessarily achieving anything. You're simply noting the thoughts you have, allowing each their moment, and seeing what further thoughts arise from them. This is very much a way of practicing your awareness skills, as you want to be objective, allowing what thoughts come to do so.

Some things you might consider in your contemplation:

- What does the word community mean to you?

- What emotions does the word community hold for you? Why?

- What are your experiences with community? Have you experienced true community? What was most noticeable in those instances?

- What are some examples of true community in your life?

- Have you had moments where you thought you were participating in community but did not have an experience of being in community?

You don't have to answer these questions. They are potential starting points to get your thoughts flowing. Each can be approached as broadly—or as narrowly—as you wish. As always, there is no right or wrong way to complete this exercise. Simply allow yourself to have an experience—in this instance, an experience of just you and your thoughts. Try to give yourself at least twenty minutes for this exercise.

Exercise 2: Discerning Your Edges—Energy Exercise

For this exercise, you will strengthen your awareness of your spiritual boundaries. Having a strong sense of these boundaries helps with discernment—a critical skill when working with spirits as it helps you differentiate between their voice, energy, and thoughts and your own internal voice, energy, and thoughts.

This exercise also helps with strengthening your sense of self, as you will be focusing on the boundaries of yourself, particularly on the boundary of your seat of consciousness, the boundary of your physical body, and the boundary of your spirit body. This helps you to better establish what is you and what is not you, affording a greater sense of presence and solidifying your presence; it helps to add definition to your very being. This is critical not just when interacting with spirits, but can greatly boost your magick, in general.

Sit or lie down comfortably. Close your eyes and center, focusing on your breathing as you did in the Scavenger Hunt exercise of Lesson 1: Witchcraft and Worldview.

> As always, please note that deliberately altering your breathing pattern may create problems if you have certain chronic illnesses, respiratory disorders, or health concerns that affect your blood pressure.
>
> Be aware of your body. If breathing exercises such as these will cause problems for you but you want to attempt them anyway, take measures to ensure your safety. Make sure you are in a safe position. You may wish to arrange pillows around you for comfort or in case your blood pressure drops suddenly and you pass out.
>
> Work with your needs. Some people have success in performing breathing exercises in working with the medications they take, timing when they do such exercises with when they take their medications.
>
> Do what you need to for you, and if safely performing breathing exercises just isn't an option, scrap them. There is no shame nor guilt in listening and responding to your body, and it does not make you a "better" or more of a "real" witch to take risks with your health, well-being, and safety.

Feel your body relax and focus your attention on the edges of your consciousness. To do this, with your eyes still closed, focus on the seat of your consciousness. This will be from where you feel you are "observing" and thinking in relation to your physical body. Generally, this tends to be about where your eyes are located, though it may be higher or lower; this is completely normal. However, it is possible to move your seat of consciousness to other areas of your body. This is a good exercise for control of your thoughts and learning to distance your spirit body from your physical body, such as when traveling to the Otherworld.

For the purpose of this exercise, you won't be taking it that far. Rather, just feel where your seat of consciousness lies. Gently extend your focus to the edges of your consciousness, to where the seat of your consciousness presses outward and then stops. Don't push past this point. Feel that distinct edge. Run your awareness along its edges, along this border. Don't try to expand that edge, just be aware of it.

Now, repeat this with your physical body. With your eyes still closed, focus your attention on the surface of your skin. Feel the expanse of your skin as it surrounds the entirety of your physical form. Feel the air upon your skin, the difference in temperature. Feel how solid and present you are, right here, in this one body. Don't focus on your insides. Keep your attention on that point where your physical body ends and something else begins. Feel this border, your physical boundary.

Then repeat with your spirit body. Feel the way it envelops your physical body and acts as an extension of your consciousness. Take care not to stretch your awareness. Keep yourself contained unto yourself. Many of us are socially conditioned to be sloppy with our energy. We may always push, always stretch and reach, search and seek, ready to take—whether that's something tangible, something spiritual, or an experience. But this tendency is to our detriment as it (1) creates unnecessary vulnerabilities when working with spirits, (2) repels many land spirits, and (3) prevents us from being truly open and able to receive because we're primed to take and to have.

Do not stretch, do not expand. Simply feel where your spirit body ends and where something else begins. Feel this spiritual boundary, run your awareness along its edges and feel how doing so enables you to strengthen this boundary without additional energy exercises, such as shielding.

Now, return your focus to your physical body and slowly open your eyes. This exercise can result in an altered state of consciousness, so it is best to avoid any tasks that require your full attention or could result in harm to yourself or others for at least an hour afterward.

Outline of Steps

1. Sit or lie down comfortably and relax your breathing. Center yourself.

2. Extend your awareness to the edges of your seat of consciousness. This is the place from which it feels like your thoughts emanate and from where you "observe" in relation to your physical body.

3. Don't push past this point, simply run your awareness along its edge, feeling where it ends and something else begins.

4. Now shift your awareness to the edge of your physical body. Keep your eyes closed and focus on the surface of your skin, focus on that point where your physicality ends and something else begins.

5. Don't focus inside your body; maintain your focus on this physical boundary point.

Alive with Spirits

6. Now shift your awareness to the edge of your spirit body. Feel the way it extends outward from and around your physical body. Take care not to stretch or expand it. You only want to feel its edge, to run your awareness along that edge and feel where it ends and something else begins.

7. Return your focus to your physical body, feeling your own solidity and firmness. Open your eyes.

Exercise 3: Being a Good Housemate

In Lesson 3: A World Alive with Spirits, you went outside and practiced awareness in a way that could have resulted in an encounter with a land spirit. This is a complementary exercise that is, in turn, focused on your awareness of your house spirits.

Just as there are circles of intimacy in regard to the living humans with whom you are in community, there are circles of intimacy regarding the spirits with whom you are in community. Your inner circle consists of those spirits with whom you are closest. This generally means your familiars (as they are spiritually bound to you). From there, the degree of intimacy decreases ever so slightly. The next circle encompasses spirit allies and ancestors. These are spirits who have a vested interest in your well-being and success, and so will work to safeguard and achieve such.

The next circle consists of the spirits with whom you share your home. If we continue from here, the next circle would include your local land spirits and other spirits that you encounter frequently but that are not within your home. Then would be a circle encompassing those spirits you are aware of but with whom you have no direct relationship and do not interact, as well as those spirits whom you know and do not want to interact with again or ever. The final circle is comprised of those spirits you do not know and have never encountered.

For this exercise, you will be increasing your awareness of the spirits with whom you share your home. Remember that your home likely contains a multitude of spirits: one that is the house and many that live within the house, some that are only found in certain types of rooms or features of the home (such as doorways), and others that wander freely. Many of these types of house spirits can be difficult to be aware of without being in that house for a considerable period of time (we're talking years) and putting in considerable effort to become aware of them. Some will do anything they can to avoid you, regardless of your effort or intent.

Keeping that in mind, you will be introducing yourself to your house spirits so as to encourage interaction with those spirits who are most interested in engaging with you.

You will need something that you can give as an offering, such as beer, bread, honey, and/or butter (these are items that tend to be favored by a variety of dominant house spirits across cultural traditions, making it likely that they will be well-received).

If you've never approached your house spirits before, consider where you may have most frequently noticed their presence. You may have noticed them (with your peripheral vision) peeking around corners at you, caught sight of hands moving quickly through doorways, or felt a sort of full or busyness in certain areas of your home. Unless this is an area that feels threatening to be in (such as a dark basement in which you know they hide), this is the area in which you should approach them.

Note that you do not need to erect an altar to your house spirits. They are far more interested in you keeping your house clean and in good working order than they are in a flat surface cluttered with objects that will need dusting.

At a time when you can ensure that you won't be disturbed for a few minutes, approach your house spirits in that area. Introduce yourself and explain why you are approaching them and what your intentions are with the house. Remember: the house is the primary concern for most house spirits so this is likely to be the only information they care about. If you are renting, tell them how you will only be sharing the home with them temporarily but that you promise to care for the home as best you can in that time. If you own the home, explain how you have accepted care for it and what your intentions are in living there (will you enjoy stable housing, raise a family, flip it in a few years; be honest). Your words should demonstrate your investment in the house and should frame your interest in these spirits from the basis of your mutual interest in the house.

Now place your offering and leave it out and in that location at least overnight. Pets, small children, and curious spouses can make this difficult or risky, so practice common sense when placing your offering.

Follow this introduction by putting your words to action and truly demonstrating your care for their home. Here after, make a conscious attempt to position that view—that you are caring for and treating your home with love—into all of your cleaning and home maintenance. And make an effort to leave them something yummy just because once in a while; there doesn't have to be a reason or occasion, after all, you live with these spirits. It's okay to show appreciation for appreciation's sake.

Talking to your house spirits when you clean or do maintenance is advised. Comment on the beauty of your home, picking out small details that you may normally not notice. Share with them what you're doing and remark how beautiful the home is as a result of the thorough cleaning job.

Most of the time, you likely won't get any sort of response or even an indication that anyone has heard you. But, over time, you may catch sight of your house spirits peeking around corners and watching you clean with more regularity and you may even find your attention drawn to things that need repair or small gifts they've left for you.

Ongoing Exercises

- Continue to work on identifying three to five local plants and three to five local trees, and finding out as much information about them as you can.

- Continue practicing feeling the energy in a variety of objects. Remember that this can be very casual and done sporadically as you go about your day.

- Continue to open your awareness in different locations. Remember not to reach or push your energy outward, you simply want to be aware of what is already there of which to be aware.

Alive with Spirits

Final Note

The efforts we take to be in right relationships with others—acting with awareness of their autonomy and personhood—is animism in action. Statements of belief only go so far; if they don't touch the way you live your life, that inconsistency shows where worldview does not exist. And one of the clearest ways that we see animism lived is through the relationships we have with those closest to us, be they living human or spirit being.

As a witch, your community includes your local spirits—the spirits with whom you share the land and your home, and those spirits that exist within the objects that fill your life. Learning how to be in right relationship with others is a continuous effort. Every bit of progress you make peels back another layer, revealing another hindrance to your efforts, as well as providing an opportunity to better understand yourself, your place in the world, and the nature of the relationship you have with the physical world. This work is difficult but deeply rewarding, and it benefits you in ways that transcend your witchcraft practice, seeping into other areas of your life. In this way, animism helps you to become a better person.

Lesson 5

The Layered Witch

There is no witchcraft without the Land, and there is no witch without a physical body. As much as animism requires us to be aware of and acknowledge the layered existence of the world in which we live, it requires us to recognize the same layering that makes us who we are. A world alive with spirits, prizing spirit beings no more or less than physically incarnate beings, includes us. We are flesh and spirit for a reason, and it is only through embracing that wholeness that we are able to actualize our full potential as witches.

So much of witchcraft is an act of seeking and finding wholeness—wholeness in the land and wholeness in ourselves. With every step we take to be in right relationship with those around us, every action to experience the world as fully as it can be experienced (embracing the physical and the spiritual), we dissolve the separation that often feels so tightly wound about us, keeping us isolated and doubting. Yet our efforts to dissolve that separation, to experience a fuller, more whole world means that we must take effort to find that wholeness within ourselves—we must include ourselves in our compassion, in our efforts to be in right relationship, in our efforts to see the layering of the spirit world so clearly upon the land, and in our efforts to reframe the way we view the land.

The Body as Place

In working to develop a deeper and more complete understanding of the Land, it is impossible to do so without taking into consideration the broader relationships happening and enacted upon the physical land. Landscape, as a term, refers to the intersection of the physical land with the culture upon it, recognizing the stories unfolding upon the land. This makes a landscape a fluid and dynamic place, one that is endlessly changing and becoming. So, too, is it the same with the witch.

A place is a site defined by relationship: the experiences you have there, the meanings and associations you have with that site, and the emotional connection you have to that site. A really great example of a place is your childhood home. It is a site filled with memories as much as spirits, a site that can elicit strong emotions even if you are not there.

Your physical body is also a place. It is a location within the physical world where things happen, where entire communities of flora and fauna live out their lives (and directly influence the physiology of the physical body, as well as influencing thoughts and emotions—things that we typically think of as part of personality). And then there are your own experiences that happen at the site of your physical body along with the layers of meaning associated with your physical body. This can include things like being disabled and the meaning and experiences that come with such—

whether that's your unique physical limitations, experiences with ableism, the relationships formed through your involvement with the disabled community, or the meaning found in disability justice work. It can also include things like race, neurodivergence, gender expression, and the ways that these things intersect and affect each other, as well as affecting the experiences that you have with other people (human and nonhuman). All these things are part of the story that plays out upon and affects your physical body, rendering it a dynamic and changing place—a metaphorical landscape for the story of your life.

There is no aspect of the world that you do not experience through your physical body. Every sensory experience, every action, every moment of your incarnation occurs in the place that is your physical body. Similarly, it is impossible to experience any aspect of the spirit world or spirituality without your physical body—even journeying to the Otherworld is not possible without your physical body. You are flesh and spirit, both, dear witch. All of you is required for this work.

Understanding the body as place alters how you perceive and approach embodied practice and, thus, affects how you relate to and understand the land as alive and spirit-filled. In Lesson 4: Being in Community, we noted that we typically play out the patterns of relationships with which we are most familiar in our efforts to forge relationships with spirits. Likewise, your relationship with your physical body impacts your relationship with the physical land—and this affects your relationships with the spirits of the land. This way you relate to your physical body has an effect on your relationship not just with the general land, but also the land upon which you live (the local land), and your capability to be in right relationship with your local spirits.

This is not to dismiss the complexities that come with having a physical body. Rather, it is an acknowledgment that the stories unfolding on our bodies are frequently similar stories to those that unfold upon the land—stories of pain ignored, autonomy denied, value delegitimized, and being viewed wholly in relation to the benefit provided to another. These stories are connected and yet they can pose a hindrance, encouraging us to center our experiences and enact similar patterns of harm upon the land as we have experienced or may be enacting upon our physical bodies. In the same ways that we may punish ourselves for the pain we have been made to endure, we may behave in similarly uncompassionate ways to the land, disregarding its needs, neglecting to mitigate harm, or even engaging in directly harmful actions ourselves.

It can be a long and painful process to work through the various associations we have with our physical bodies, to untangle the many stories and work to be in right relationship with ourselves. But our efforts to be in right relationship with the land can help us to undertake that healing for ourselves, help us to untangle the stories of pain, lack of autonomy, or pressure to meet impossible standards that our physical bodies hold, and instead begin creating new stories founded in efforts to be in right relationship with ourselves. This is a process of healing and working towards wholeness. It helps us to see how living *is an inherently spiritual practice*. As the literal vehicle through which all spiritual experiences are had, the physical body is no less sacred than any other part of the land, than any other place in the landscape that impacts and informs our lives.

Seeking Embodiment

As witches, we are at our most powerful when we work from a place of wholeness of ourselves. Attaining this wholeness requires us to recognize that we are not "spirits having a physical experience" but flesh and spirit both for a reason. Each is equally valuable and important; each serves a purpose in our existence and deeply impacts how we experience life, the world around us, and other people. Scorning one for the other does nothing more than create an imbalance of ourselves, resulting in a distinct block that prevents us from accessing our full capabilities and available power.

You exist as physical body and as spirit body, both essential to who you are, both integral for you to be alive, both occupying the same space time and directly contributing to your experiences and your well-being. And it is with your spirit body that you firstly and primarily interact with—and experience—energy and spirits. Because of this, the use of psychic or spiritual skills is dependent upon the ways that you have learned to identify the physical (and mental/emotional) sensations that correspond to the sensations your spirit body experiences. This is because there is no way to separate your spirit body from your physical body so that what you experience with one will not also be experienced with the other (the separation of one's spirit body from their physical body is commonly referred to as death, which illustrates how foundational to the way we experience existence this connection between physical and spiritual is for us).

Consider how you feel when you have a cold, the flu, or a bad chronic illness day: you may feel tired, you may have trouble concentrating, you may be in pain, you may be irritable, your thoughts may be scattered, and you may even snap at people around you. All of this impacts your capacity to do any sort of magick or make use of your spiritual skills. Why? Because just as the physical experience is affecting your thoughts and emotions, your spirit body is also affected.

The same way that physical health concerns can affect you spiritually, concerns with your spiritual health can affect your thoughts, emotions, and physical body. You exist as all of these, together as one—not as a collection of parts but as a series of layers. Strengthening your awareness of the layering that exists in the world around you—physical world and spirit world sharing the same space, spirit people and physically incarnate people sharing the same space—begins with strengthening your awareness of this layering that is so integral to your own existence.

Witchcraft is an embodied craft. It is born of the physicality of the land and its practice demands that we recognize the value and beauty of the physical because it cannot be practiced without such. That witchcraft roots us more firmly within the natural world and also requires us to embrace our own physical nature is no coincidence, for it is in operating from that place of oneness of ourselves, standing firmly within the knowledge and power of our physical bodies and spirit bodies, that we are able to wield greater power in both the physical world and the Otherworld. Through cohesion of the self, we are more formidable and better capable of building and maintaining the connections we seek through spiritual practice—in this world and the Other.

Embodiment is not so much a prioritizing of physical over spiritual as it is a recognition of physical body as a place where spiritual experiences occur and the means of our being able to have those experiences in the first place. For the witch, embodied practice involves the many ways in which we seek spiritual experiences through purposeful use of our physical bodies. It is the physical body utilized not so much as a tool but as the foundation of action for the spirit body and as the site of spiritual experience.

Breath work for the purpose of shifting your state of mind in order to facilitate energy work, as you've experienced with centering and grounding, is an example of embodiment. Altering your behavior and the way you live your life so as to better reflect and facilitate your growing awareness of the world as thrumming with spirits and consciousness is another example of embodiment. This is you changing the way your physical body moves through the physical world, thus changing the experiences you have and are capable of having in addition to changing the experiences you have with the spirit beings you encounter.

There is no way to have a spiritual experience, to work magick, or to interact with spirits that does not involve your physical body. This naturally means that embracing the necessity of that union, seeking the wholeness of physical body and spirit body conjoined, adds a layer of potency to the magickal action you're undertaking. So much of what we do as witches is bound up in the inclusion of the physical body, as well as the use of physical objects in order to facilitate interaction with spirits and the spirit world. This is a part of what inscendence means for us as witches: it is the ways in which we entangle ourselves in the Land through seeking and finding wholeness between the physical and spiritual, and that entangling is inherently embodied practice.

Becoming a Place of Liminality

Through embodied practice, when you work from a place of union of physical body and spirit body, you become something more. The body as place takes on a new quality, that of alterity—otherness. It becomes a place of liminality: where the separation of the two is dissolved and you become a bridge that unites physical and spiritual. You become the space in between and so the two (physical world and spirit world) become one through you.

You can choose to step further into this liminality and use it as a means of actualizing some of the more poetic aspects of witchcraft. Trance is a vehicle for slipping deeper into liminality—a means of shifting your focus from the rational to the unknowable, from the physical to the spiritual. It is how you remove yourself from a world of firm rules and limitations and how you enter a world of opportunity and potential.

When you enter trance, you enter that place of wholeness of the world and wholeness of the self. You dissolve the separation that exists between the two, allowing the spiritual to be just as prominent—if not more—than the physical. Unsurprisingly, it is for this reason that trance is so commonly employed within witchcraft.

In simplest terms, trance is an altered state of consciousness. An altered state of consciousness is any state of mind that is not your most frequent state of mind. In the context of witchcraft, trance is the ways that altered states are used to magickal ends. It's how you get your thinking brain out of the way so that your spirit body can be more prominent. It is how you move your seat of consciousness out of the mental/emotional and into the spiritual via the physical. Yet trance needn't be deliberately sought. Its presence isn't a requirement to the working of magick. Rather, it is a part of how you—as a multilayered being—function. Trance is a natural and inherent part of what humans experience when working magick, an identifiable type of sensation that corresponds to the deliberate working of magick. And so, we seek to facilitate trance because we will enter a trance (if only a light one) regardless and leaning into how we operate facilitates the working of magick.

Everyone experiences multiple occurrences of being in an altered state every single day. This has nothing to do with magick being oppressed in society or magick being the things science doesn't understand, but instead everything to do with the way humans work, regardless of personal neurology, because consciousness is inherently fluid and changing. As witches, we can—and do—make use of that fluidity.

Examples of common altered states of consciousness:

- zoning out when bored

- becoming engrossed in a book when reading

- listening to music and losing yourself in the song

- runner's high

- singing in a group

- taking a few deep breaths to "calm yourself"

- sleeping and dreaming

- meditation and mindfulness

Just as altered states of consciousness are very common in everyday life, they are also incredibly common in witchcraft. When someone discusses being in a "proper state of mind" to work magick, they are talking about entering an altered state of consciousness. These states, depending on the steps you take and what you are trying to achieve, can vary in their depth. By "depth" what is meant is the degree to which your focus is pulled away from the physical. For example, a "deep trance" typically means you are less responsive to the physical world. You won't hear most noises going on around you, you likely will not notice temperature or lighting changes; your focus is firmly placed elsewhere.

In trance, with focus shifted away from the physical, it is easier for your intuition to come through. Similarly, it makes it easier to perceive the subtly around you, such as sensing or seeing energy or local spirits. Because of this, a lot of basic things in magick utilize a trance state—and many more advanced skills depend on experienced use of trance states.

Examples of ways trance is used in witchcraft:

- divination

- spellcraft

- spirit communication

- healing work

- journeying

Notice how these are pretty standard witch things. That's how ubiquitous trance work is in this craft. It's a quirk of how humans function that we use to our benefit. Trance feels big and kind of scary, but it's really that common—both in frequency and remarkability. However, that it is common and that we each do experience altered states every day doesn't mean that deliberately using trance for witchcraft is necessarily easy or won't require practice to be able to wield successfully.

Effective trance work—especially for spirit communication, healing work, and journeying—is dependent upon strong discernment skills. In this case, we are absolutely talking about your skill at telling *this* from *that*. Strong discernment skills require a strong sense of self, this is your awareness and knowledge of yourself, your ability to discern you from not-you.

In Lesson 4: Being in Community, you began working on developing your sense of self through the Discerning Your Edges exercise, wherein you confronted the boundaries of your consciousness, your physical body, and your spirit body. Any action that you take to better understand who you are—and who you are not—helps with strengthening your sense of self. This includes things like being aware of your baseline emotions, so you know what is unusual for you. Or knowing the general pattern and nature of your thoughts, including what your thoughts feel like, so you can better distinguish authentic spirit communication from your imagination trying to be helpful and create an experience for you.

In addition to strong discernment skills and a strong sense of self, effective use of trance is also facilitated by strong skills in awareness (so you can feel the energy changes within you) and energy work (so you can encourage those changes and, if need be, lean into the process to encourage trance, especially if you are trying to take it deeper). Repetition and practice are important: learning how to do something better through the act of doing it over and over again.

Exercises

For this lesson's exercises, you will build upon your efforts to strengthen your skills in energy work and discernment. These exercises may seem difficult, at first glance, but they are based in actions you have already been doing, taking that familiarity and stretching it in a new direction. This may give you clues to ways that you can further stretch that familiarity and apply foundational skills to more complex magickal actions. Through repetition and applying foundational skills in new ways, those skills only grow stronger, making their use second nature to you and your magick feel more instinctual than planned. You'll also be doing a progress check, making some assessments of how things are going and freewriting in regard to impact and action.

The first exercise is an energy exercise to help you feel the layering of your spirit body and physical body, as well as to strengthen your sense of self (in an energetic/spiritual sense). Once you have the basic actions down, definitely experiment with this exercise in a variety of situations as it has a variety of applications (including protection).

The second exercise can be completed in three separate blocks of time, if you wish. Each block of time should take between ten and thirty minutes, with more time (potentially) in the third block of time due to comparing your experiences.

The third exercise is the progress check. It centers around a handful of questions to get you considering your experiences in working through this book, as well as the impact you've had on the world around you up until now. There is a lot of room for exploration and tangential introspection. These prompts could easily become a focus for you over a number of days, if you are the journaling type. Regardless, try to spend at least twenty minutes thinking about these questions.

Exercise 1: Defining your Borders—Energy Exercise

Part of having a strong sense of self is being in control of yourself. In this context, it is far less your ability to keep your thoughts in order or your emotions in check than it is your ability to not be sloppy with your energy. When you are sloppy with your energy, you are not in control of it. It leaks and flows, it reaches and touches. Your energy becomes intrusive to others (especially spirits) but also becomes susceptible to others, such as parasitic spirits and parasitic living humans.

Knowing how to keep your energy contained allows you to strengthen the edges of your spirit body, strengthening that border of yourself. And when you can better discern the edges of your spirit body, you can better feel the layers of yourself and the way they overlap.

For this exercise, you will be consciously moving energy through your spirit body and along its edges. This exercise is very similar to the grounding exercise you did in the previous lesson yet differs in mechanics and thus result, as you will not make a complete energetic circuit. You will be pulling energy from the earth up through the bottom of your channel (an energetic space that runs the length of your spine and along which energy flows), moving it up through your channel, concentrating that energy out through the top of your channel, and then directing that energy to flow down across your skin before pulling it back up through the bottom of your channel.

Typically, this yields a stronger sense of spiritual awareness, with your psychic skills heightened, but with a clear sense of separation between you and outside spiritual forces. It should take you about ten to twenty minutes to do the first time, five to ten minutes thereafter. Don't worry if this exercise is difficult to do the first time. Try to move through the steps; keep your focus on pulling that energy up and moving it up and out of you. It may take a few tries before you can complete the action smoothly.

Sit comfortably with your spine as straight as you can comfortably manage. Close your eyes and relax your breathing, engaging your diaphragm so that each inhalation is deep and even. Once you are centered, as you inhale, pull energy from the Earth up and through the bottom of your channel. This is located at about the area of your perineum. You may feel your pelvic floor muscles relax or stretch.

Bring the energy up to the level of your heart and exhale, holding the energy there. As you inhale, pull more energy up from the Earth and through your channel. Keep the energy moving up past your heart, past your eyes, and, as you exhale, direct that energy out the top of your channel—located at your crown. Don't send it out in a burst, instead direct that energy out gently, allowing it to flow along the outside of your physical body, washing down and over you.

Now when you inhale, pull this very same energy back up through the bottom of your channel. Do not pull more energy from the Earth: cycle the energy you've already pulled. Move the energy up through your channel and out through the top as you exhale. Again, allow the energy to flow along your skin and down.

Repeat this movement of energy until it becomes comfortable to maintain. When you are ready to stop, there is nothing further needed to do than to no longer move the energy. It will dissipate on its own.

Outline of Steps

1. Center.

2. Inhale and focus on drawing energy from the Earth up through the bottom of your channel.

3. Bring the energy to the level of your heart. Exhale and hold the energy there.

4. Inhale and draw more energy from the Earth up through your channel, moving it past your heart.

5. Exhale and direct the energy out through the top of your channel (top of your head).

6. Direct the energy to flow gently downward along your skin.

7. Inhale and pull this same energy back up through your channel.

8. Move the energy up through your channel and out again, allowing it to flow along your skin.

9. Repeat the movement until it's comfortable to maintain.

Exercise 2: Entering Trance

Remember that trance is a very normal part of being human, so entering trance is fairly easy to do. For this exercise, you will experiment with a variety of simple methods of entering a light trance. Note that there is no risk to you in entering a light trance. You naturally move through multiple states of consciousness every single day, with many of those states being comparable to what you will achieve with this exercise.

This exercise is in three parts. You may wish to do each part at a separate time in order to plan your time better and squeeze more witchcraft into a busy day, as well as to allow yourself a fresh starting point for each. Should you repeat this exercise, you may find that you get different results should you do each part in succession rather than spacing them out. As always, feel free to experiment as part of increasing your knowledge and sense of self.

You may wish to take notes for each part, this will make it easier for you to compare results and figure out which methods work best for you at this time.

Part One:
Identify an activity that you love to do and don't need to focus on very hard to do it. This could be something like dancing, crocheting or knitting, painting, hiking, yoga, anything in which you can engage and lose yourself. Do the thing you love and let yourself fall

into the moment. Remember that feeling, write down what it feels like so you can revisit that sensation and compare it to other activities. Be sure to consider how you felt physically (were you acutely aware of your body? Did it feel distant?), how you felt emotionally (were you content, distracted, or did you experience euphoria?), mentally (were your thoughts sharper, fuzzier, or absent?), and spiritually (did you feel larger than your physical size?).

Part Two:
Experiment with the following simple ways to enter trance.

- *Breath Work.* Position yourself comfortably and close your eyes. Breath in through your nose for a count of four and then exhale through your mouth for a count of five. Do this for a few minutes. Then open your eyes. How do you feel? Remember this feeling. Record that feeling. This is what you've been doing when you center. Consider now the subtle differences it affords you and the ways you've noticed it impacting your ability to feel energy. Remember, too, to consider how you felt physically, emotionally, mentally, and spiritually. This is also a good time to consider differences in your experiences now compared to when you first centered in Lesson 1: Witchcraft and Worldview. Has there been a change in how sensitive you are? Have you noticed differences in the quality or type of sensations you experience as a result of centering?

- *Swaying or Rocking.* Sit comfortably, this could be in a chair or it could be on the floor with your legs crossed or tucked to one side. Close your eyes, calm your breathing, and begin swaying side to side or rocking back and forth. Your movements should be smooth and steady; your thoughts should be calm and generally focused on your breathing and movement. You could mentally count your breathing (for example, inhale and count one as you rock forward, two as you are upright again, three as you rock forward again, four as you sit upright, and then repeat as you exhale). There is no need to move quickly, just steadily, rhythmically. Do this for several minutes; you may wish to set a timer on your phone. Afterward, think about how you are feeling and what you felt while doing this. Record your observations, especially noting how you felt physically, mentally, emotionally, as well as spiritually.

Part Three:
Compare your experiences in doing the activity that you love and the two trance techniques. How did the state of mind achieved while doing the thing you love compare to the state of mind achieved when you deliberately sought to enter trance? What similarities did you notice? What differences did you experience? Which of the trance techniques that you tried was most effective? What was different for you with that technique compared to the others? How did it compare to the activity you love?

Exercise 3: Progress Check—Journal Prompt

Already, you have done so much in working through this book to help stretch your skills as a witch and to see the world around you in new ways. You've practiced energy exercises that have potentially had you moving energy in new ways, helping you discover new applications on your own. You've taken direct action to better familiarize yourself with your local land and even begun building important relationships with the spirits with whom you share your home. And you've done quite a bit of valuable contemplation regarding the impact your witchcraft has on the way you live your life, the extent to which you're meeting your goals as an animist, obstacles (and how you might resolve them) to living more fully as an animist, and experiences you've had that influence your ideas and expectations in regard to community.

This has truly been a lot to take on and potentially more than you can fully process at this point. That's okay. There is no rush and you can revisit all the exercises in this book as you so feel drawn to do—with it being strongly recommended to do so once you've fully worked through this book and have had time to more fully process your thoughts and integrate your experiences into your practice and life.

For now, however, it's time to do a quick progress check. As with previous journal prompts, you will be freewriting, and so your writing can take any form you wish. You may feel moved to write a few thousand words, or you may find making a succinct list to be the best approach for you. There is no right or wrong way to complete these prompts so long as you allow yourself adequate time to consider these questions and your responses.

Consider the following questions:

- In thinking about everything you've done so far—the energy exercises, the journal prompts, the moments of introspection based on what you've been reading—how have these things impacted you?

- What has proven to be the most challenging? Why? What have you found to help with minimizing or supporting yourself in this challenge?

- What do you feel has had the greatest impact on you so far?

- Are there any areas in which you find yourself consistently struggling? What can you do to better support yourself?

- What has been the biggest surprise for you so far? This could be regarding an experience you had with a certain exercise (maybe you had stronger results than anticipated, maybe something you've never done before was much easier to achieve than you expected) or even something with your ongoing work of getting to know your local area.

- Being completely honest with yourself, how have your life and your witchcraft impacted the world around you up until this point? Are there changes that need to be made in your practice so that your actions are in better alignment with your values and worldview?

Ongoing Exercises

- Revisit your list of obstacles from Lesson 2: Witchcraft Comes from the Land. Make any necessary adjustments to your list. Note your evolving thought processes regarding some obstacles. You may wish to note reasons why some obstacles no longer are obstacles for you.

- Continue to work on identifying local plants and trees, and finding what information you can about them. Be sure to take notes and cite your sources for future reference.

- Revisit any of the energy exercises with which you may have struggled. You may also wish to revisit some exercises to see the progress you're making. The more complicated energy exercises you've been doing now will have an effect on your experience doing the earlier energy exercises and you may find them to be much easier to complete now.

Final Note

As an animist, you are defined by the relationships you cultivate with those around you. Yet the quality of those relationships is impacted by the relationship you have with yourself. As much as there is no witchcraft without the physical land, there can be no witch without the inclusion of the physical body. Through embodied practice, you uncover another layer of experience that is possible within the world. Greater depth of meaning reveals itself and in moments of awe, where wonder and amazement dominate your thoughts, the connection that naturally exists between you and the Land becomes palpable. Through embodiment, you take direct action to dissolve the perceived separation of physical and spiritual, allowing yourself not just to see the wholeness that exists between your physical body and spirit body but to see that same lack of separation existing so fully in the world around you—a wholeness between the physical world and the spirit world. From that place of multilayered wholeness, the things that you are capable of achieving as a witch can only grow larger.

Lesson 6

The Layered World

A common name for the spirit world is the Otherworld, with the word "other" emphasizing the dissimilarities between it and the physical world. Given those dissimilarities and Western society's obsession with compartmentalization, the spirit world is typically thought of as existing elsewhere—and, admittedly, is often presented through a Protestant Christian lens, bearing considerable similarities to the common understanding of heaven. Unsurprisingly, understanding of the spirit world—including its location—differs greatly through an animist lens.

Rather than existing elsewhere, there is no separation between the spirit world and the physical world: they are layered upon each other, existing in a state of wholeness in much the same way as we all exist as physical body and spirit body, together and one. Due to the nature of physicality and living as physical beings (not to mention that societal influence to ignore the spiritual in all forms), our attention is not always drawn to the ways these two worlds overlap. Yet as we cultivate and hone the skills of witchcraft—skills like sensitivity to energy and spirit presence, or the ability to enter trance—that lack of separation between the worlds becomes more evident.

The witch exists in the intersection of that dual liminality—this layering of the world and the layering of the self. Understanding and bridging these layers is a foundational premise of our work: we are mediaries between the worlds, operating with a foot in both due to conscious action to function from a place of wholeness, wherein our physical body and spirit bodies work together, as one. From that place of wholeness, we are able to traverse both worlds—the physical and the spirit world—gaining insight and experience to the workings of both.

Layered: Together and One

When we think of the land and nature, we have a tendency to think of the things that fill nature. We think of plants, trees, animals. Rarely do we consider the "empty spaces"—the dirt, the rocks, the wind—except in relation to those other living, animated things. But this is something that more bleak and desolate landscapes, such as deserts and steppes, teach us intimately. Only an outsider would visit them, look at the open expanse and scattered plants looking dry and crispy, and call it a wasteland. One who lives there, one who has done the work to belong there, knows how vibrant and alive such places can be, how full—and complete—they are in their own way.

This isn't to assert that any one type of landscape is better than another but, rather, to underscore that different things are different and that's good. More to the point here, this further illustrates that the influences we carry with us when approaching the land are far deeper, far broader than we might first realize. There is strong temptation to approach all landscapes through a filter based on those landscapes with which we're familiar. This is a common behavior, as it is through looking for similarities that we find connections for understanding and for security—and this is true regardless if we're talking about adjusting to a wildly different environment from that which we were raised in or whether we're talking about adopting a new religion or worldview than that with which we were raised.

The search for familiarity in the disparate is to be expected but it, too, is a hindrance as that searching can limit your ability to see the differences that define that landscape (or worldview), to see and accept the differences. It can keep you trying to reconcile differences for which there is no reconciliation (not all things are compatible; as you've been discovering throughout this book, the community-centered approach of animism contrasts sharply with the individual-centered approach of contemporary Euro-American society. The differences cannot be reconciled, but they can be navigated). This can keep us from fully accepting and appreciating that landscape for what it is, as the pursuit of finding familiarity keeps us comparing one location to another—holding that location to a standard that may very well make no sense.

Being able to be within a location and to hold the awareness of it as unique—appreciating the differences that are an intrinsic part of its beauty, personality, identity, and basic nature—is essential in order to grow your awareness of the spiritual qualities of that place. By "spiritual qualities," we're talking about the spirits that live there, the non-human people whose stories play out upon that landscape without most living humans being aware. This is knowledge you can have as a witch, however. But it requires an awareness and appreciation for the physical components of the land first.

From there, you will begin to see the way that the spirit world does not exist separate from the physical world but, rather, the two exist in the space, layered—in the same way that your physical body and spirit body are layered and together make you who and what you are. That very same layering within you of physical and spiritual is the reality for our world, with the physical and spiritual existing together. As noted in Lesson 2: Witchcraft Comes from the Land, "There is no spiritual connection with the Land without a physical connection to the land."

Traversing Spirit Heavy Locations

There are some locations where the layering of the spirit world atop the physical world is more readily apparent, where spirits are more easily seen and that touch of Other is more easily felt. These spirit heavy places can be interesting to pass through, as the greater number of spirits making their presence known means that there is an increased chance of having some sort of interaction with a spirit. Keeping in mind that some land spirits are very dangerous, this makes it important to take precautions to better ensure safe passage through these spirit heavy places.

Navigating these spaces isn't necessarily complicated, but it does require you to act like a witch: to acknowledge the awareness you have of the obvious layering of the spirit world in that place that comes to you because of your skills as a witch, to use those skills in a way that protects you just as much as in a way that acknowledges the presence and autonomy of the spirits who call that location home, and to use those skills in a way that demonstrates that you understand that you are a guest in that location.

What does that mean?

It means putting everything you've learned into practice: acting in a way that reflects your understanding and awareness of animism as a reality and practicing good manners.

Oftentimes, these spirit heavy places can be discerned by a distinct boundary. This can be something like the edge of a forest, a river dividing the land in two, a fallen tree across a path, or two large stones that form a natural sort of doorway. There is nearly always some sort of physical feature that corresponds with the edges of that spirit heavy place, especially if you are traveling on any sort of path or trail.

Crossing such a boundary can be used as a way of journeying to the Otherworld (which can be done solely with your spirit body or it can be done while you are still rooted in the physical; we'll discuss journeying in more detail in the next section). There are some basic precautions to take when entering these spirit heavy locations in order to ensure safe passage and better protect yourself from any spirits who might respond to your presence in a hostile manner. These precautions apply when journeying but also when you are simply out hiking and encounter a spirit heavy place.

- Have a means of securing your safety and ensuring you can get home again. This can mean carrying ritual tools on you such as a stang (a ritual tool used to aid in journeying to the Otherworld, which is especially helpful as it allows for travel in and out), a blade (for defense), a blasting rod (also for defense), or walking stick (also for defense). Specifically, while journeying, you may wish to have something that serves as a touchstone on you. This can be something like a stone, statuette, piece of jewelry, or bone, that you hold in your hand. If you need to return to your physical body quickly, you can turn your attention to that object in your hand, causing it to appear within your hand in the Otherworld and calling you back to your body.

· Ask permission to enter. While all physical objects contain a spirit, and there are spirits that exist without physical form yet move freely about the physical, there are spirits who are guardians of places. In Lesson 4: Being in Community, we noted how your house is filled with various spirits, including a spirit of the house itself—this spirit would serve as a guardian spirit of that house. So, too, are there guardian spirits for locations, such as a forest, meadow, arroyo, mountain, or sea. These spirits are most easily noticed at the boundaries of the area they safeguard. It behooves you to ask them for permission to enter the area they safeguard. They may not grant you safe passage, and ignoring that can lead to a variety of unfortunate situations befalling you— such as you losing your keys, getting lost, getting injured in some way, or having some sort of terrifying experience.

· Act accordingly. Showing respect to the guardian spirit is in your best interest as they may keep more surly spirits from noticing you. It also demonstrates that you understand you are a guest, and is a way of acknowledging the right those spirits have to that area (after all, it is their home). This is part of being in right relationship with these spirits. So if you approach the boundary of a location and you very clearly hear the guardian spirit tell you that you are not welcome to enter (perhaps only at this time, perhaps ever), respect their words—both because spirits have a right to consent and because that lack of permission may be based on matters of which you are unaware and may pose a risk to you (such as a rather cantankerous spirit being active that day and your entry not permitted so as to keep the two of you from interacting).

- Pay attention. You may encounter other spirits while passing through these areas. Be respectful and take care not to damage the physical area. If you are told not to travel a certain direction, follow that guidance. Your presence may not be desired in certain places or you may be being guided away from beasties who lack patience for living humans. If you are told not to touch certain plants (or anything at all), follow that advice and touch/take nothing.

- Acknowledge help offered to you. When you exit the area, acknowledge the guardian spirit's role in your safe passage. If you have water on you, pouring some onto the ground can be an acceptable offering. If you have none, spitting (reverently) onto the ground and sharing your saliva (water from your body) can be respectful. Do not leave physical objects behind, such as ribbon tied to trees or coins left at the base of a tree—these items are nothing more than litter, regardless of your intent (tying items about trees can also cause harm to that tree by restricting its growth and movement, and potentially damaging the bark and introducing pathogens that could kill the tree). Food items should also never be left behind as they will be consumed by wildlife. If it cannot already be found naturally occurring in that place, it likely doesn't belong there. Remember that whether your actions are respectful is based on the impact of those actions—not your intentions.

Walking Between the Worlds

There are places within the physical world (as well as the spirit world) where the overlapping of the worlds is palpable. These are areas of the natural landscape that serve as "portals" to the spirit world, meaning that they are places where the ability to pretend that separation exists between the worlds grows weak. These are energetically potent places, the effects of which cause you to shift into that state of witch awareness almost instinctively. As a result, you may see spirits more readily in these locations, you may even feel them more strongly—particularly spirits who may otherwise generally ignore living humans. You may be more apparent to these spirits just as they are to you, as a result of that shift of awareness, and so they may find it more difficult to not notice you in these locations

Potential examples of such places include:

· natural clearings

· naturally occurring arches, formed by rocks, trees, brush, and so forth

- anywhere water meets land meets sky

- edgeways and fence lines

- paths leading into a "wild" area

- forked trees

- two or more trees growing near to each other but in such a way as that they create the impression of a doorway

- quick moving water, such as a river, stream, creek, and especially seasonal streams and arroyos

- some seasonal ponds and forest pools

These locations can be used to more easily journey to the spirit world, too. While this isn't actually a form of spirit travel, per se, it is a means of harnessing that effect of these locations to more strongly shift your awareness from the physical world to the spiritual world. This allows you to walk about the physical world as your awareness is focused on the spirit world, allowing you to essentially experience both worlds at the same time. This is called world walking and is, admittedly, a more advanced technique. We won't go into the specifics of how to do this in this book, as its execution is dependent on a number of prerequisites that each take time and effort in order to become competent at them. (These include not just the seven foundational skills of witchcraft, but also skills like trance, spirit communication, and journeying to the Otherworld.) However, know that this a direction you can absolutely explore and the things we cover in this book will help to develop the foundation to be able to do so.

> Journeying is one of many names for the practice of traveling to the spirit world. It is also known as traveling, spirit travel, spirit flight, sending the fetch (however, this term also applies to a very different practice as there are multiple perspectives on what a fetch is, with one perspective using it as another name for the spirit body and another as a name for a familiar like spirit, for example), and astral travel.
>
> Regardless of name, the technique is ultimately the same: you shift your awareness so that it is focused on your spirit body more strongly than your physical body and, through that focus, you cross the boundary into the spirit world—as you'll experiment with doing in Exercise 2: Slipping through the In-Between.

However, when speaking of journeying or spirit travel, it is an action that largely takes place in trance and is done via spirit, that is, your physical body remains motionless and your spirit body is the prime vehicle through which you move and with which you interact with spirits and the Otherworld. As you can likely tell, this makes discernment skills very important because your initial efforts to journey are pretty much guaranteed to not be real—they will be your imagination enthusiastically trying to help you have an experience. This is something that happens for everyone because the successful doing of witchcraft is dependent upon cultivated and honed skills, not natural ability. With time and practice (specifically, practicing trance techniques, building your sensitivity to energy, developing your intuition, and strengthening your discernment skills) it becomes easier to let go of expectations of what it is you're supposed to be experiencing so that you have a genuine spiritual experience.

Ultimately, why any of us do anything in regards to witchcraft is entirely up to us individually. Just as we each come to witchcraft for our own reasons, everyone will have their own motivations for why they do what they do, regardless if what they're doing is something rather pedestrian—like making incense—or incredibly woo, like walking between the worlds.

Nonetheless, there are some practical reasons why you might want to journey to the Otherworld:

- facilitate communication with certain spirits (this is especially useful if you need to acquire information or are bartering a deal with a spirit; the barriers are removed between you and that spirit, regardless if those barriers are spiritual or mental/emotional)

- develop and practice new magickal skills (energy exercises work differently in the Otherworld but they do still work and they work in a way that can make it easier to practice those skills in the physical world)

- discern who is in a particular physical location with you (such as when you know there are heavy spirit presences in an area, you can tell there isn't anything blatantly dangerous, but you can't get close enough or catch a good glimpse to see who is there; journeying to the Otherworld makes it easier to tell who is there with you)

- it's badass (you're an adult: why you do what you do is on you. If you want to travel to the Otherworld just because it sounds cool, you are absolutely within your rights to do so.)

Obviously, most of these things are more appropriate to Otherworld travel, where you aren't moving between the worlds while anchored and moving within the physical world but more so moving energetically through your thoughts and spirit travel. But it's worth remembering that leaving your body is not necessary for walking between the worlds when operating within an animist worldview due to how palpable the layering of the physical and spirit world is and our ability, as beings with similar layering, to experience that layering as a state of wholeness.

This form of travel—where your spirit body alone journeys—is facilitated by visualization. As we noted in Lesson 1: Witchcraft and Worldview, visualization is a rather terrible name for a complex skill that involves the full sensory recreation of a place, object, or situation. More than imagination, visualization is the way in which you bring your mental and emotional faculties together with your spirit body in order to accomplish magickal action, the same way you bring your physical body and spirit body together in order to accomplish a magickal action. Visualization is a way for you to shift your focus and attention away from the physical and gently prime yourself to experience that which you are trying to experience. Unlike how that may come across, this doesn't create the experience for you (journeying is not an act of imagination), rather, it is a way of focusing your spiritual awareness onto that which needs to be focused upon so that way you can experience what is there to be experienced.

For example, in journeying to the Otherworld, you may begin by visualizing yourself at a natural portal that you found in your local area. Perhaps you found a portal formed by an outcropping of rock that forms a ledge stretching over part of a trail. You visualize yourself standing before this outcropping and then passing beneath it. When you emerge on the other side, you find yourself in a completely different location than where the outcropping is in the physical world, perhaps you find yourself standing beside a small creek at the edge of a meadow.

In this way, visualizing yourself at a familiar physical location didn't create an experience at that location as it would if you were imagining. Rather, that sensory recreation allowed your spirit body a way to connect with that physical location and to access the energetic component of that natural portal, using it as a means of journeying to the Otherworld. Using a familiar location or natural portal is not required in order to journey, however, it can be a helpful and effective way for you to begin developing your journeying skills.

Exercises

Our exercises continue to build upon the experience you've been gaining throughout this book, helping you to hone your skills and develop a bone-deep understanding of the mechanics of the basic actions within those skills. For this lesson, you'll be applying your growing energy work skills in a way that is similar to the energy exercise you did in the previous lesson, yet produces a very different result. If you struggled with the Defining your Borders exercise, it's okay to jump straight into Exercise 1 without revisiting that exercise beforehand; they are similar enough that doing one will help your ability to successfully complete the other. This exercise should take five to twenty minutes to complete.

For the second exercise, you will be performing a very basic and safe journeying, traveling to the Otherworld in order to begin developing familiarity with the process. It's recommended to try to do this exercise at least twice; the first time may take as long as an hour but it will get easier with practice. For the third exercise, you will be revisiting the location that you visited in Lesson 3: A World Alive with Spirits, to further develop your relationship with that location.

Exercise 1: Shielding

For this exercise, you'll build off the basic structure of the Defining your Borders exercise of the previous lesson, where you moved energy into, through, and out of your channel. That exercise is essentially a containment practice, helping you to keep your energy contained rather than leaking about you or wandering off and being pushy when you're trying to respectfully acquaint yourself with a new place. However, for this exercise, you will be using that energy to create an impenetrable energetic barrier about you, offering protection from energy being sent at you both consciously and unconsciously.

Sit with your back as straight as you can comfortably manage. Close your eyes and center. Allow yourself to relax, both physically and mentally.

Inhale and pull energy from the Earth up and into your channel. Bring it to the level of your heart and exhale, holding the energy within you. Inhale once more, pulling more energy up, bringing it to and holding at the level of your heart as you exhale. Do this a third time, pulling energy from the Earth up through the bottom of your channel, up to the level of your heart. Feel the impression of expansion as you hold that energy and exhale.

Now, a fourth and final time, pull energy up from the Earth and into your channel. Pull it up to the level of your heart and keep the flow moving up and through you. Feel all the energy you've been holding move up and out through the top of your channel. As you exhale, bring the energy out through the top of your channel and bring it down around you, not along your skin, but several inches out around you. Weave the energy about you so that it encases you in a tightly-woven net, shimmering and electric, that closes fully beneath you.

As you inhale, do not pull energy but, rather, move your personal energy along the inside of this net, sealing and hardening it. Exhale and continue the action. Continue to breathe slowly and evenly as you sit within your energetic shield.

In growing more proficient in energy work, it can be helpful to think of energy as being either internal to you or external, as the mechanics of working with one versus the other can involve different steps. That internal energy is commonly referred to as personal energy while that external energy (when not coming from a direct source, such as the Earth) is commonly referred to as universal energy.

Throughout this book, you have been using techniques that have equipped you to work with personal and universal energy. This exercise, the containment exercise of the previous lesson, and the grounding exercise in Lesson 3: A World Alive with Spirits have all been helping you practice accessing and manipulating universal energy.

> In Exercise 2: Push and Pull, of Lesson 2: Witchcraft Comes from the Land, you made energy balls that you then absorbed through your face. Use that same technique for working with personal energy in this exercise; you can raise your hands to direct the energy if helpful, making a gentle sweeping motion (palms out and fingers touching—mitten hands not glove hands) a few inches out from your body.

This shield will expire on its own, the energy naturally dissipating. However, you can take it down by gathering up personal energy, holding it tight and blade like, and sending it forward from your seat of consciousness and into your shield, cutting it so that you can peel it back. In doing this, the energy will quickly dissipate as it falls away. This action can be accompanied with physical movements—extending one hand to slice the shield, breaking it, and then sweeping your hand along the shield's edge to pull the energy back into you—to make it more embodied and potentially easier to accomplish. Experiment and see which works well for you right now; you may find this changes with repeated practice.

Outline of Steps

1. Center.

2. Inhale and focus on drawing energy from the Earth up through the bottom of your channel.

3. Bring the energy to the level of your heart. Exhale and hold the energy there. Do this three more times.

4. Inhale and draw more energy from the Earth up through your channel, moving it past your heart.

5. Exhale and direct the energy out through the top of your channel (top of your head).

6. Direct the energy several inches out around you and weave it into a tight net, shimmering and electric, that completely encloses you.

A Variation:

Another way to effectively shield is through the common ritual practice of casting a circle. This technique comes to us from ceremonial magic via the popularity of Wicca. This is a highly simplified version of the circle casting performed in both, yet it achieves similar results in that it creates a sphere of energy about you, keeping that which is out out and that which is in in.

Stand or sit comfortably. It is advised to leave your eyes open, the better to strengthen your ability to see energy. Hold your hands before you, palms together. Breathe evenly.

Now, project energy through your dominant hand, creating a ball of energy between your hands. When you can feel the ball strongly, open your hands and hold your dominant hand before you. Moving your hand clockwise about you, project energy so that you trace a circle about yourself.

As you complete the circle, see the energy expand to create a glowing sphere about you, shimmering and electric, impenetrable and strong.

Like with the variation above, this circle will dissipate on its own, however, you can cut it open, using the same technique above or by piercing it with your hand and pulling the energy back into you as you move your hand counterclockwise about you.

Outline of Steps

1. Hold your hands before you, palms facing each other.

2. Project energy out through your dominant hand and create an energy ball.

3. Continue to project energy into the ball as you open your hands and draw a clockwise circle about you with your dominant hand. Visualizing the energy as electric and pulsating about you can be helpful.

Exercise 2: Slipping through the In-Between

Full sensory recreation is what distinguishes visualization as a potent magickal exercise and tool from that of make believe or day dreaming. This is an important distinction to make because real magick isn't happening just in your head. It is the cooperation of your mind, your physical body, and your spirit body to effectively wield energy that is essential to work magick. Take one of those things out of the equation and you're just going through the motions.

Visualization is a skill that requires consistent practice in order to develop and make it be of any real use. Ideally, this or similar visualization exercises should be done repeatedly in any one week in order to help build your skills. Aiming for at least five minutes, two to three times a week, will be far more effective than spending more time visualizing but only doing so once a week or once every few weeks. Repetition truly makes the difference here, especially if your visualization skills are developing.

As visualization is also an effective way to set parameters for the movement of energy and spirits, for this exercise you will be visualizing yourself before the boundary to the Otherworld—effectively creating a neutral space at the edge of the Otherworld to which you can later journey in order to practice energy exercises and even interact with local spirits who are not bound to physical objects. This space is a liminal space, a quiet location in which you are unlikely to encounter spirits without seeking them. It is a staging ground, a place that exists just outside the border of your thoughts and at the edge of the spirit world. It is a real place yet is a place you can alter and can trust to be relatively safe within, and also somewhere to where you can travel as part of journeying (heading to this neutral space and entering the Otherworld through it).

It is irrelevant that the boundary between the physical world and Otherworld may or may not appear as you visualize it: you are purposefully creating a mental/emotional construct to serve as a mediary space so you can more easily begin engaging with the Otherworld and become familiar and comfortable with your spirit body being more dominantly active than your physical body. The exact visual details do not matter as whatever you visualize will still provide the desired energetic framework necessary to this action.

Sit or lie down comfortably, ensuring that you won't fall asleep and that you are in a safe position if you do. Close your eyes and center, as you have previously done.

Once you have centered yourself, begin creating the following scene within your mind. It is perfectly fine if you find yourself deviating from the following description. What is most important is that whatever location you are visualizing, you do so with the utmost detail. Even if you find yourself visualizing some place different, as long as there is that definitive boundary and you are able to immerse yourself in that visualization, you will still attain the full benefit of the exercise.

You stand in a meadow. Tall grasses and wildflowers sway gently as the breeze rises and brushes across your skin. The sky is heavy with clouds. There is threat of rain that you can smell and that creates a stillness across the land. It invokes a sense of heightened alertness within you.

The meadow stretches far in every direction except right before you. Not more than ten yards before you stands dense and heavy woods. Sentry like trees reach high while the edge of the woods is a tangled mess of undergrowth. Shrubs, immature trees, and native plants reach outward to the meadow, competing for sun and space. The heavy scent of rotting leaves and organic matter reaches you on the breeze. It is a fertile, though imposing, forest.

You are alone in the meadow with the forest dark and tangled before you. It is quiet but for the faint twitter of birds among the trees and the clicks and whirs of insects in the meadow.

Do not approach the woods. Do not leave the meadow. Just stand where you are, feeling every last detail of this scene. Feel the decisive edge where forest and meadow meet, feel the boundary. Know you could approach it but now is not that time. You are not prepared. For now it is enough to see it, to feel it, to know that it is there and able to be reached again as easily as you have reached it now.

When you have finished, end the visualization by sweeping the scene away, leaving your mind blank. Open your eyes and draw attention back to your physical body. This exercise can create a slight change in your state of consciousness so be aware of how you feel and are interacting with the world. Avoid activities that require your full concentration, such as driving or cooking, until you are certain you have returned to your usual state of consciousness.

A Variation:

You can experiment by using one (or more) of the trance techniques you practiced in the previous lesson as a means of facilitating journey work. Center, then perform that trance technique, and then begin your visualization.

Note that this may result in a more intense sensory experience, as you will be in a deeper trance than if you perform this journeying as written above. This shouldn't create any complications for you, but it can make for a more vivid experience and may require more after care (such as drinking water, eating a salty snack, avoiding activities that require your full attention, letting others know that you may be a little out of it for a few hours and to help keep an eye on you).

Exercise 3: Seeking an Experience, or Not

For this exercise, you will be revisiting the location you visited for Exercise 3: To be Aware from Lesson 3: A World Alive with

Spirits. In that exercise, you wandered about a particular location in a state of open awareness, allowing yourself to more effectively experience . . . something. You might have felt nothing, you might have felt winding currents of energy through that space. You might have seen nothing, you might have caught flashes of light or movement out of the corner of your eyes that felt suspiciously like . . . something.

What might or might not have happened is not important so much as that you held yourself in a state devoid of expectations so that something *could happen*; after all, just because you go outside doesn't mean you're guaranteed an intense spiritual experience. With that in mind, you will be revisiting that location in order to practice your awareness but now with greater knowledge of the kinds of things that could be there to be experienced—or possibly with ideas of why things you experienced before, like perhaps seeing/feeling a shimmering around an opening in the brush, caught your attention in the first place.

Before you enter the location, remember the presence of a guardian spirit of that location. You might not have felt any indication of their presence on your previous visit—and you might not now—but make a point of addressing them and asking for permission to enter and for safe passage. You may wish to center before gently extending your awareness along the boundary of this location and addressing the guardian spirit. You may feel a strong response to your request, you might not feel anything (we'll go over some of the intricacies of communicating with land spirits in Lesson 7: Communication, Interaction, Manners, for now it is enough to be aware that communication can happen, that it can take many forms, but it is never guaranteed).

Enter the location and find a place where you can sit comfortably. Close your eyes, calm your thoughts, center, and gently extend your awareness. At first, just focus on the immediate area about you, the ground beneath you, the air touching your skin. With each inhalation, extend your awareness further, allowing yourself to open fully, feeling for what may or may not be. Feel without expectation. Just be, just breathe, but be gently aware.

As you continue to hold yourself in that place of receptivity, take note of what you feel. Are there any areas near you that feel particularly interesting? Is there a spot where the trees lean just right that makes your witch-senses tingle? Or a patch of brambles that looks . . . different from the rest of the area? Do you feel any natural currents of energy, perhaps following a line of trees or naturally placed stones?

Such places may come into your awareness with a tingle, a sense of warmth from afar, a gentle yet strong tugging at the center of your being. Such a place may greet you with a shiver, a flush across your skin, or a feeling to leave. Take note of the full scope of these sensations and the emotions and physical responses they evoke in you.

Slowly get up and begin to wander about the location. You can carefully approach any of these places that caught your attention, or you may simply continue to make a mental note of any places that feel different or that fit the descriptions of potential portals to the Otherworld (as noted above). Some places might not have any physical indications that they could be portals, yet there might be a feeling of more about them.

Record your observations in your notes for future reference.

You may wish to repeat this exercise at different times, such as during the day, at night, or during one of the liminal times of dawn or dusk. You may notice differences in how some places feel, you might not notice anything different. But you won't know unless you try and, regardless of what you experience, what you feel in that location will help you to better understand this location and the potential it holds to you as a witch.

Ongoing Exercises

- Revisit your list of obstacles, noting your progress and making any necessary adjustments.

- Revisit your work on identifying local plants and trees. Have you made a point to sit with these plants and talk to them yet?

- Practice your energy exercises. They are remedial, yes, but skill only grows stronger with practice. The energy exercises you've been practicing are useful when interacting with spirits, when traveling through spirit heavy places (really good time for that containment exercise . . .), and for supporting the skills necessary for journeying to the Otherworld.

Final Note

So much of the work we do as witches centers on teaching ourselves to have an unbridled experience, carefully peeling back the layers of how we once saw the world so that we may see with eyes unclouded. In working toward reclaiming the wholeness of our-selves, our actions are most effective when also working to discover the wholeness of the world about us. In this way, we find that the separation we thought so clearly existed between the physical and spiritual is the same separation that has been forced between us and the Land, keeping us isolated and unaware of the community that was always there and available to us.

The witch's place is in the liminal, especially the liminality that is created through contradiction. For in seeking wholeness, we become something more, something other. We become liminal our-selves, a means for wholeness to move through us, rippling outward and affecting change as much as any spell we might cast. Yet just as any spell is limited through the use of physical tools, all actions of the witch are limited through the use of our physical bodies. This is our poetry. Our ability to access the spiritual is dependent upon the physical—and this is as true for our physical bodies as it is for land.

Lesson 7

Communication, Interaction, Manners

The actions we take to interact, communicate, and build relationships with spirits are the basis of spirit work. In Lesson 1: Witchcraft and Worldview, we noted that spirit work is animism in action—it's the way that your awareness of the reality of a world alive with spirits turns into acknowledgment and alters the way that you live your life and practice your witchcraft. More than any other trait of witchcraft, spirit work is often approached with the most trepidation and frequently is an area where the most baggage comes up, like in the way that we noted in Lesson 4: Being in Community that we tend to repeat patterns of relationships with which we're most familiar with spirits in our efforts to interact and build a relationship with them, for better or worse.

So much of interacting with the spirits around you is dependent upon your ability to be aware and to be responsive. Actively engaging in spirit work challenges assumptions about what spirits are, how they behave, and what is possible in regard to communicating with them. It is truly an area where the only way to really learn is by doing. Yet there are general points of guidance that can be detailed. Throughout this lesson, we'll be covering those generalities in a way that will prepare you to begin actively interacting with your local spirits. These experiences will help you more fully embody an animist worldview.

When the Land Speaks

The benefit to the witch in building relationships with spirits is profound, but being able to do so is predicated on recognizing that the spirit world does not exist for us. We may call ourselves witches and understand spirit work to be inseparable from witchcraft, but if you approach any spirit and expect them to acknowledge you simply because you are a witch then you will find out just how little worth the ideas of living humans hold with spirits. You are on a path of building relationships with these people, and as is true with human companions, right relationship is not formed through exploitation or extraction.

It is essential, as a witch, to recognize spirits as people and their presence in the world as no more remarkable than your own. This attitude helps you to avoid approaching them with entitlement (that is, "you have to help me, I'm a witch and I said so!"), with delusion (that is, the spirit told you to go away but you're so focused on how spirits and witches are best friends that you didn't even notice and just continued like they were actually helping you), or with fear (that is, you relinquish the not-insignificant power and capability you hold as a witch and approach the spirit as if they are omnipotent and omniscient, occupying a position of power above you).

And, in doing so, you allow yourself the ability to enter into relationship with them—not all of them, that would be weird—but a small number who you will know as much as you know anyone else in your life. Some you will know because you see them and say hello each day. Some you will know by name and where they live. Some will know your name and where you live. Some will know all your secrets and keep them safe.

Communication with spirits can be active or passive. With active communication, you are purposely seeking to communicate with that spirit. Passive communication, on the other hand, does not involve direct action on your part. Rather, that direct action is taken by the spirit.

> Active communication involves you seeking direct contact and communication with a spirit. It requires the cultivation of skill to be able to reach out to them, communicate with them, and discern a response.
>
> Passive communication involves a spirit seeking to communicate with you. It requires you to be open to that communication, to be aware of your surroundings so you notice the indications, and to be aware of the sensations you feel and the thoughts that come unbidden that denote a spirit communicating with you.

Active communication typically involves the use of tools, such as divinatory tools, or direct communication (where you rely entirely on your spiritual/psychic skills). Ritual techniques can also be involved but are not necessary; they are aids that amplify, but they are not required in order to communicate with land spirits, house spirits, or the spirits in objects.

With many spirits—particularly the kind that we've been focusing on, who are bound to a physical object or a physical location—direct communication is the only way that you can communicate with them. And you must be in proximity to that spirit in order to interact with them in any way. Attempts to use divination to communicate with these types of spirits will only yield information *about them*, not from them, and that is not communication.

For example, you cannot communicate through divination with the guardian spirit of a specific mountain just as you cannot communicate via divination with me. How could I manipulate the tool? How could the mountain manipulate the tool? In order to use divination as a form of spirit communication, that spirit must be present with you so they can manipulate the physical objects you're using for divination. Part of spirits being real (and witchcraft being real) is that there are rules to how all of this works. That means that there are limitations. There are things that simply cannot happen regardless of how convenient it would be for us nor how much we intend for them to happen.

Likewise, passive communication—where a spirit deliberately tries to communicate with you—can take a few forms but it is also subject to limitations due to the nature of these spirits. One such form passive communication often takes is that of signs and synchronicity: little moments that stand out as being filled with something more. That "something more" is a defining trait because it isn't the event that catches your attention that is important so much as it is the energy that fills that moment and that conveys a feeling of otherness to it. It's that energy that carries meaning because it is the active force that has caused so many little things to come together in such a way as to make an otherwise unremarkable occurrence feel noteworthy.

Signs and Synchronicity: Cautions and Clarifications

Signs and synchronicity are not quite the same thing but are two different occurrences that help demonstrate awareness of your inherent connection to the world around you (including the energy currents actively moving about) and the way that impact can, and does, ripple outward from you as well as inward toward you. In this way, both are defined by the energetic presence surrounding their occurrence more so than the assignment of numerical value or correspondence.

A sign is generally any sort of occurrence to which meaning that does not exist inherently within that context can be assigned to that occurrence. For example, say that you are lost in thought while driving, running through the details of a rather stressful situation that you're currently going through. You look up and see a billboard with an image of a snake on it. You feel your concerns momentarily dissipate and feel that the snake is a sign that you need to take decisive action, that there is greater threat in the situation than is apparent.

While no one can conclusively confirm for anyone else whether something is a sign (they were neither there to feel the energetic currents and patterns surrounding that moment nor would that energetic presence behind the sign cause the defining spiritual sensations in them because it is irrelevant to them personally), something like this could very well indicate a genuine sign.

This is where discernment skills become essential because they help you determine if there is anything more behind that moment (that is, clear energetic presence behind the occurrence that you feel in similar ways to feeling a spirit presence or a portal to the Otherworld). That something more must be spiritual—as in your spiritual skills tell you that there is a spiritual element to that occurrence. Without that spiritual element, you run the risk of assigning meaning that isn't warranted. Sticking with our example, you could feel that there was something significant about the moment, but not have any spiritual indication of such. So you do as one does: you search online for "snake spiritual meaning." And . . . you get a dozen plus websites with correspondence lists citing multiple "meanings" for snake, with everything from danger to rebirth to fertility to chaos noted. Which "meaning" is the right one for your sign? None of them. The meaning exists in that moment (interpreted by your practiced skills) or it does not exist.

This applies similarly to synchronicity—repeated occurrences that happen in relatively close succession of each other yet have no apparent connection to each other. Often, it is stated that something is not a sync unless it occurs a minimum of three times. But just as there is no universal "meaning" to a snake, there are no firm rules that dictate something is important only with X numerical value attached to it. "Meaning" can only be personally determined and is largely influenced by personal experience and culture.

Complicating the issue further is that there is widespread overestimation of synchronicity within the broader witchcraft community that frequently comes down to the bias of perceiving relationship between two (or more) unconnected situations based on no evidence existing outside of one's mind (that is, the desire for spiritual experience creates a connection and inserts meaning). This creation and assignation of meaning is also a form of apophenia, where the repetition is seen as demonstration of meaning with no other evidence suggesting such.

And if that weren't enough, our brains are literally wired to help us perceive what we want to perceive in the world. This is called the reticular activating system and its entire job is to prime you to see what you want to see and experience what you want to experience by causing you to discard sensory input that is contrary to what you want. When you find yourself looking for signs and synchronicity to help you solve a dilemma you're facing and then you encounter numerous syncs pointing to the exact answer you're hoping for, that's your brain doing its job and not a spiritual experience.

Developing the basic skills of witchcraft (awareness, discernment, discipline, focus, energy work, Will, and visualization) is essential so that you know what energy feels like and how you respond in the presence of strong moving energy currents and spirit presence. These skills are how you feel the energy surrounding that potential sync and how you trace that energy outward from the sync and along the thread of your life, showing you that it is a spiritually significant moment. These skills are also how you more clearly recognize the absence of spiritual sensation in these moments and the need to step back and attend to your emotions because they're distorting your perspective.

Pattern recognition is an amazing thing and can be quite useful in life (as many neurodivergent people can attest), but it is not an effective means of determining spiritual significance behind something. Only the use of developed spiritual skills can provide such confirmation.

But, again, there are limitations. Land spirits will not communicate with you through signs and certainly not through synchronicity unless you are in proximity to them. They can't. Just because they are spirits does not mean that they can affect everything about us on a whim. They are subject to limitations due to their non-physical form just as we are subject to limitations due to our physical form.

Shufflemancy is never going to play you a song to deliver a message from a river spirit. You're not going to encounter mentions of deer throughout your day as a message from the guardian spirit of a forest. You're not going to see pictures of acorns everywhere because an oak tree wants to talk to you. These examples are impossible because they are outside of the realistic capabilities of these types of spirits, these spirits cannot make these events happen for you just as you cannot consciously make these events happen for someone else.

However, there exists potential for communication in that strange liminality of dreams. Just as trance (an altered state of consciousness) can lend itself to journeying to the Otherworld, dreaming involves a variety of altered states of consciousness that can be conducive to magickal application and, thus, spirit communication.

In general, we can sort dreams into three types:

- dreams: (deliberately lower case), imagery created by your brain based on things you were exposed to recently, things that have been occupying your thoughts, and strong and frequent emotions you've been having, as well as other things your brain supplies due to the influence of hormones, sensory stimuli while you're asleep, (for example, sounds, lights, needing to use the bathroom, and so forth), and because human brains tend to seek new stimuli, and so will create or modify stimuli.

- Dreams: with that purposeful capitalization, these are dreams that have that distinct feeling of more about them. They may be prophetic; they may feature clear spirit presence and communication.

- journeying while asleep: these may begin as lucid dreams but don't always. You may find yourself traveling to a neutral location or directly to the Otherworld. These types of dreams are distinguished by that feeling of something more but also by your ability to be fully aware. You may find yourself instinctively using magick in these dreams, such as forming energy balls and hurtling them at perceived threats.

Spirit communication is most likely to occur during Dreams or while journeying in your sleep. It has been hypothesized among witches that Dreams may take place in a neutral location or they may occur in their own specific location called the dreaming that is similar to the Otherworld yet is distinct. Your own experiences will help you to discern where you may—or may not—be going when in Dreams, based on your form, angle of observation, and specific experiences that unfold. Nonetheless, there is a liminality about Dreams that does allow for spirits to seek and interact with you in that space. If you are in near enough proximity, some land spirits can reach you in this place—such as wandery spirits that live in a forest that surrounds your house, these can easily approach you in your sleep to make use of the increased ease of communication.

Yet just as it is far easier to find "signs" and "syncs" when you go looking for them, most of the dreams you have will be little more than mental chatter that your brain supplies to entertain you while you sleep. This isn't to diminish the wonder that can come with dreams but to highlight the defining characteristics of genuine signs, synchronicity, and spirit communication in dreams so that you can better distinguish these remarkable experiences when they occur—and to encourage you to do the work to develop your skills so that you experience them more regularly.

Reaching Out

There is no standard formula to follow to begin a relationship with a spirit. This is because, as has been stressed throughout this book, spirits are people. Just like if you were trying to make friends with another living human, how you approach that person, how they respond, and what unfolds as a result will all vary. Nonetheless, there are some generalities that can be made based on the type of spirit with whom you are approaching.

Generally, the simpler the type of spirit (for example, inability to communicate in complex ways, such as impressions of colors versus words and sentences; being bound to a physical object; inability to travel long distances; and the like), the safer they are to approach as their potential to cause harm (serious or otherwise) is minimal. Remember, most spirits want nothing to do with you. But there is still a big difference in approaching and befriending the spirit of a potted peace lily and approaching and befriending(?!) the type of spirit that crawls across rooftops at night in cities, causing the streetlights to flicker and dim one after another (witch tip: you don't approach these spirits).

The more complex the spirit is, the more you have to let them lead and, often, the more effort you will have to expend to get their attention and convince them that you are worth their time. This you would do through first respectfully approaching them. If they are a type of spirit who is bound to a physical location or object, you must be near that object or location for them to hear you. You can put a "symbol" on your workbench for the spirit of a river, but that spirit can't hear you unless you are at its banks. You can have a branch from a large alder tree before you, but the spirit of that tree still can't shuffle those Tarot cards through you and influence which cards you draw.

As noted in the previous section above, for a spirit that is not bound to a physical location or object, techniques like dream work and journeying to the Otherworld can be quite useful as they are means of slipping into liminality and sinking yourself deeper into the spirit world, this may make it easier for you to approach and speak with that spirit. This lesson's exercises will help you to practice the skills necessary for doing such.

Once you have approached that spirit, familiarity must be established. This means that you will have to approach them multiple times. And each time you do, you have to give them a reason not to ignore you or to tell you to go away. What exactly that is, you'll have to figure out based upon that spirit and the experiences you have when interacting with them. This could involve removing garbage from around their home (for physically bound spirits) or leaving them gifts. What kind of gifts? Something that would be appreciated by them. For physically bound spirits, anything more than water is ill advised as any physical objects you leave hold greater impact than use, or meaning, to those spirits and are nothing but garbage left outside. For a spirit you're approaching in the spirit world, gifts that hold energetic weight can be left. These can be objects that you have in the physical world that you take with you, give to them, and then destroy by fire once you return to the physical world, for example.

From there, you have to pay attention and be responsive to that spirit. So much of what you do now will be to continue to build familiarity with them, to feel each other out, and talk with each other. This is absolutely not the point where you ask them to help you with your magick or to be your familiar (in the cases where you're interacting with a type of spirit where such a relationship is possible, such as the spirit of a deceased animal whose spirit lingers close to their remains). But to do so, when that familiarity has not yet been established, is not only insulting but also betrays ignorance. And with spirits, you can bet that any time you show yourself to be foolish, that foolishness will mete a response. Intimate relationships take time, this is as true for friendships and romantic partners as it is for a spirit you would have as an ally.

Discerning Genuine Spirit Interaction

There can be a lot of uncertainty when you first begin to communicate with spirits because you are still strengthening the skills necessary to not just have those interactions with spirits but to also tell the difference between a genuine experience and wishful thinking. But there are some things that you can do to help yourself as you continue to strengthen those skills. These are ways of practicing discernment (in the sense of telling this from that) in a way that is practical and keeps you grounded within this work.

Test your assumptions. While a big part of strengthening your skills requires you to trust those skills, it's okay to get a second opinion on what you may—or may not—have experienced. You can do this by:

- doing divination for yourself

- running things past another witch (preferably one with experience in spirit work because someone without that experience can't really help except to validate your emotions)

- divination by an experienced witch (preferably a spirit-worker as their whole shtick is serving as a mediary between living humans and the spirit world; they're better equipped to see definitive signs of confirmation or refutation)

Pit your experience against common sense. Consider if there are everyday explanations for what happened. Did you see a pair of crows on your way to work, but overlooked the fact that it's mating season and they have a nest in the area? Did a leaf happen to hit you in the face but you were walking outside on a windy autumn day? A little bit of skepticism is healthy—witchcraft does not ask you to take anything on faith, what it does ask is that you do the work to cultivate and hone skills that allow you to have direct experiences. And those direct experiences will show you what is possible, what isn't possible, what is happening, what is not happening. But anything that witchcraft shows you to be true will not go outside of common sense. Remember, common sense is not equivalent to a materialist worldview.

Try to repeat the experience. If you are really uncertain of what happened, can you do the same things and get the same or similar results? One of the defining traits of witchcraft is that of ritual—

steps that are repeated because they bring consistent results. Ritual is a deceptively simple practice that is part of how witchcraft shows us how the world really is; the fact that ritual is possible shows us that there are rules to magick, the fact that there are rules and that we can repeat steps and get generally predictable results shows us that we aren't making this up or acting from a place of belief or faith. So, if you have an experience as a result of doing x, y, and z, and then you repeat those steps and get a similar result, it is safe to assume that your original—and second—experience was genuine.

Exercises

While working through this book, you have worked hard to strengthen your spiritual skills so that you can experience the world—and yourself—in a way that is fuller and more complete. You've been carefully developing your awareness, your focus, your ability to feel and move energy, and your visualization skills. These skills are crucial in being able to recognize and interact with the layering of the spirit world atop the physical—things that are necessary if you are to take animism from an admittedly neat concept and turn it into a worldview that touches every aspect of your life.

The exercises, this time, are more adventurous than previous exercises, but are well within your capabilities to complete. The first is a three-part exercise, so you may wish to split it up in order to make better use of your time. Each part should take ten to twenty minutes to complete. For the second exercise you will be journeying, this should take thirty to sixty minutes to do. And the third exercise is a journal prompt (with a slight twist) that should take twenty to sixty minutes to complete.

Alive with Spirits

Exercise 1: Seeking Interaction

No relationship is possible without an introduction. So, for this exercise, you will be attempting to interact and communicate with three different local spirits. What types of spirits you introduce yourself to is up to you, however, you will gain more from the experience if you try to interact with a variety. It is highly advised to stick to spirits who are bound to physical objects and locations (as we've been focused on), as there are different skills required and precautions necessary with spirits who are not bound to physical objects or locations. There is also considerable difference in the way that these spirits communicate in comparison to each other. It's worth going slowly and beginning with spirits who are generally likely to be amenable to your presence and your efforts to communicate with them.

For example, you could try to interact with one type of land spirit (maybe the spirit within a plant or tree in your yard, that you pass by frequently, or that caught your eye during Exercise 3: Seeking an Experience, or Not from the previous lesson), one type of house spirit (sure, you could leave this general, or you could seek the small spirits that hang out in doorways or the spirit you might have caught peeking at you behind corners), and the spirit of a particularly old object that has interacted a lot with living humans and with whom you have familiarity.

Remember that there is a difference between feeling the energy within an object and feeling the presence of a spirit. This is not an exercise in psychometry. This is an exercise in becoming more familiar with the feeling of a spirit presence and the ways in which that spirit—that person—may choose to communicate with you.

Center yourself and perform the containment exercise from Lesson 5: The Layered Witch. Approach the physical object to which that spirit is bound, but do not touch them. If they are bound to a location, such as the guardian spirit of a place, place yourself at the boundary of that location—just at the edge and at a place where a human or animal may naturally, and comfortably, enter.

Take a moment to appreciate what you see, note the natural beauty of that object/location. Carefully, without touching anything, extend your awareness and your energy toward them. Take care not to push. You want your energy to approach in the same way that you hold your hand out to a cat you don't know yet want to befriend. Pay attention to any indication that your approach is unwanted. If you should get such indication (which will be most likely from a land spirit), withdraw immediately and try with someone else.

Draw physically closer to them as you also make your energy more prominent to them. If you are connecting to a spirit bound to an object (be it a stone, plant, tree, or antique table) gently touch them with one hand. If you are connecting to a spirit of a location, place your hands—palms down—upon the ground (if this isn't a feasible action for you due to physical limitations, viable alternatives are to hold one hand toward the ground or to close your eyes, inhale slowly, and as you exhale stretch your spirit body toward the ground and toward the boundary of that location). Pay attention to any indication that your presence has been noticed, or acknowledged. Remember, if you get any indication that your presence is unwanted—especially if you feel a strong or hostile response—withdraw immediately. Respecting the personhood of a spirit means respecting their autonomy and right to say no.

For now, it is enough to stop here, allowing yourself to note any sensations you may have that indicate you've been noticed. You may feel pressure at your brow or the back of your skull, or even a tingling across your arms, or the feeling that every pore on your body is wide open. There are a lot of possibilities here; make note of them and what you feel. If the spirit encourages conversation with you, absolutely pay attention and respond, holding yourself open (don't let your enthusiasm for communication cause you to close yourself down) and remembering to be respectful and withhold expectations for what may or may not happen.

When you are ready to stop and leave, thank the spirit of that object or location for allowing you to spend time with them and begin pulling back slowly, doing the above steps in reverse: express your gratitude for the spirit allowing you to spend time with them (you don't have to speak or think a thank you, gratitude can be expressed clearly as an attitude and in your demeanor), pull back physically, then slowly pull your energy back to you and hold yourself contained again.

Record your experiences and compare them for each type of spirit.

Outline of Steps

1. Center and perform the containment exercise from Lesson 5, Exercise 1: Defining Your Borders (pull energy up through the bottom of your channel, send it out through the top of your channel, direct the energy to flow along your skin, pull the same energy back into you through the bottom of your channel, keep the energy cycling this way for a few moments).

2. Approach the physical object or location to which that spirit is bound. Take a moment to appreciate the beauty of that object or location.

3. Carefully extend your energy so that it lightly touches them. Pay attention for any response; act accordingly if you're told to back off.

4. Draw physically closer: touch the object or place your hands on the ground. Pay attention and act accordingly.

5. Do not announce yourself or make any sort of declarations. Focus on this interaction and on any indications you may have that your presence is noted or acknowledged.

6. Repeat for two other types of spirits. Record your experiences and compare.

Exercise 2: Seeking the Otherworld

For this exercise, you will build off the journeying that you did in the previous lesson. Where previously you journeyed to a neutral place at the edges of the Otherworld, this time you will travel past that border and in. You'll do this by journeying to the location that you previously visited in Lesson 3: A World Alive with Spirits and in Lesson 6: The Layered World, as you have been gradually building greater familiarity and intimacy with this location. Now it's time to begin taking that growing relationship further.

Note that you do not need to be physically present at that location to do this exercise. In fact, your physical presence there would be counterproductive and would not yield the same results.

If for some reason you have yet to choose a location and begin visiting it in order to do the two previous exercises, you can still perform this exercise, however, you will need to choose a location with which you are quite familiar. Ideally, the location you choose should have minimal human influence, that is, a location that is more "wild" and left to nature's devices is a better choice than a location with many buildings. This location should also be one that you know well—you should be able to recall enough details that you can visualize it clearly, using that visualization as the stepping stone for your spirit travel.

Center. Perform any trance techniques that you've found to be effective. Now, visualize the meadow at the edge of the forest that you visited last lesson in Exercise 2: Slipping through the In-Between. Take your time to build the scene, as this will help to pull you into trance and make journeying easier: see the tall trees before you, feel the wind on your skin, hear the birds.

When you have the scene recreated, approach the edge of the forest. As you approach the boundary, see the trees part, exposing a narrow path through the deep shadows of the forest. Stick to the path. Feel the cool soil on your feet, the chill of the sun-parched air on your face.

Walk the path, one step at a time. A light slowly appears before you. It's the other side of the forest. The path is taking you straight to the light. You continue to walk. As you reach the other side of the forest, the trees again part to let you through.

On the other side of this forest is the location you've been visiting (or the familiar location you're using as a stand in). Take a moment to observe all the details. It should appear very similar to the way you experience this place in the physical world. When you are certain it is the same place, you can begin to explore. Wander about slowly, holding yourself open and aware. Pay attention to your surroundings. Watch for things that are different.

When you are ready to leave, turn back to the forest. Approach the edge, watching as the trees once again part, exposing the same path that you traveled through the forest to get here. Take the path back to the meadow.

Once you've reached the meadow, begin turning your attention back to your physical body. Wiggle your fingers and toes and then slowly open your eyes. Record your experience and any differences in the location that you may have experienced. You may wish to sketch a map and mark specific places so you remember to explore them in the physical world to better compare and contrast your experiences in visiting the physical and spiritual layers of this location.

You may find yourself remaining in an altered state of consciousness for a few hours after journeying. Be gentle on yourself. Avoid doing anything that requires your full attention in order to be safe (no cooking, no driving, or the like). It is advised to get something to drink and to have a small snack (salty foods can be particularly helpful; hold yourself to any necessary dietary requirements).

Exercise 3: Record Keeping—Journal Prompt

If you have been following the guidance to take notes of your experiences in working through the exercises, and jotting down thoughts you have while reading, you will have amassed quite a bit of valuable information that helps you with better charting your progress and with better understanding yourself and how you function, spiritually (which is helpful for strengthening your sense of self). However, because you're human, because life happens, your notes may be a beautiful disaster. It's time to go back and see if you can straighten things out a bit.

Revisit your notes, adding things that you might have forgotten to initially include and realizations you've had in retrospect. This is also a great time to make new entries regarding the progress that you've been making with the exercises you've been practicing—maybe you've noticed new sensations when you practice the discernment exercise from Lesson 3: A World Alive with Spirits where you've been comparing the energy of three different things. Or maybe you've had new experiences that feel connected to previous experiences, such as a series of unusual events after your last visit to the location with which you're building a relationship (recording those experiences now could prove helpful in discerning future experiences).

This is a good time to also double check that you didn't miss completing any exercises, as some exercises had multiple parts and some lessons might have had more exercises than you could easily juggle at that time. You may also wish to add better organization to your notes, such as ensuring each entry is dated, perhaps even making a note of the lunar phase in an effort to make it easier to later spot potential patterns and the effects such a prominent natural cycle has on you.

Additionally, you may wish to revisit sections of this book where you found yourself feeling the most resistance or confusion.

With the benefit of new experiences where you've been interacting with the Land, traveling to the Otherworld, and otherwise engaging in some serious witchcraft, these sections may strike you differently now. Recording your thoughts now—as well as clarifying your resistance or confusion and how they were resolved—can be an invaluable source of information to have available to you later.

Ongoing Exercises

- Revisit your thoughts on community (from Lesson 4: Being in Community). Note any places where you find your thoughts and impressions around the concept changing.

- How are your efforts to increase your familiarity with your local area going? Have you identified a variety of trees and plants? Have you done research to understand their nature and general disposition?

- Revisit any previous exercises that you may have struggled with initially. Alternately, you may wish to revisit earlier exercises in order to gauge your progress and see how your skills are growing stronger.

Final Note

There is something about recognizing the world as alive with spirits, recognizing that these spirits are generally benign and just doing their thing, that helps make things click on a deeper level. It is as if a switch gets thrown within your head and suddenly things—witchcraft things—just make more sense. You see and feel the energy currents swirling about you more easily. Your magick becomes more potent. Your confidence in your abilities multiplies. The old folk tales begin to speak to you on another level and you hear the whispers on the wind. You hear the moonlight as it passes through the canopy and meets the forest floor. You feel the turning of the seasons within your bones. You begin to truly see the world and live your life as a witch and as an animist.

Lesson 8

The Witch within the World

There is so much about witchcraft that defies glamorization—remaining steeped in smoke, covered in dirt, and attentive to the unfolding patterns around us. As you've been experiencing first-hand, this craft is rarely flashy. The foundation seated firmly upon the Land and the web of connection that extends so much further than is clearly discernible, the work of the animist witch is quiet, contemplative, and frequently engaged in conversation with the numerous spirit beings with whom you share this world.

The truth of any worldview is evident in the actions of the one who holds it. Witchcraft remains a way of being within the world—a system of magick that provides tools and protocol for moving through a beautifully layered world filled with variation in being and potential modes of existence. This is a trait that sometimes comes through more clearly than the inherent inclusion of animism as its worldview, yet in both cases, it is the same: an animist and witch are known through their actions. It is impossible to stride the boundary between the worlds—to live in a way so as to dissolve that separation, to forge deep and personal relationships with the spirits about you—and not have the basic flavor of your life reflect such. And how wonderful that is, how much for the better life is made for living in awareness of the connection you share with the Land.

Dissolving Separation

The deeper one digs into animism, the stronger the focus on wholeness and connection becomes. What is it to value relationships and community except to see the way that we are intimately connected to others? What is community but the manifestation of the bonds among many people? At every point, within every context, animism demands that we discard the illusion of separation that we've been told exists. It demands that we consider ourselves in relation to others (including ourselves; who are you in relation to yourself is a pertinent question to ask when working to be in right relationship with yourself . . .). And it demands that we consider the full picture—every component, every person, every aspect—as being integral to the whole and to a more complete understanding of what something is, be that something our place within the world or the very cosmos itself.

A driving force within spirituality, as the personal expression of one's relationship with the Greater All, is that of the search for connection. We yearn for a sense of belonging, of being a part of something bigger than ourselves, for connection with something larger than ourselves that will provide a sense of stability and help us make sense of our existence. Even within the highly rebellious and transgressive practice of witchcraft this remains true, as so many of us come to this craft in search of greater meaning for our lives and a way to feel less isolated—less separated—from the world.

Much of how witchcraft is currently generally presented (be that broader realistic depictions in media or even in the dominant representations within our community) seeks to dissolve this separation by reframing aspects of the Western worldview that contribute to separation in the first place. A great example of this is the strong consumerist current and the prioritizing of aesthetic over substance. These things come with a rush of feel-good emotions that temporarily make us feel better, make us feel like we're part of something (particularly in the witchcraft scene, after all, if you own the things that witches own, that means you must be a witch, right?) but they do nothing to create a lasting sense of connection, nothing to dissolve separation nor to help us heal from the pain and trauma of living within that separation for so long.

When you act, as a witch and within an animist worldview, your actions necessarily reflect your pursuit to dissolve separation and to find wholeness within yourself and within the world, to not just seek but to find that connection with something more— with others, with the land, and with the many spirits around you. And that lack of separation becomes more evident not just within your everyday life, but within your magick. It can be found in the increased awareness of how your physical body affects your spirit body, impacting the ease of using the basic skills of witchcraft, and also in the ways that your spirit body affects your physical body, emotions, and thoughts. It can be found in the way your magick becomes stronger, as you are no longer working within a false paradigm that places you in battle against immovable forces, fighting to achieve what you desire. Instead, your magick flows more smoothly, with fewer obstacles and can reach so much further as a result of the far reaching connections nurtured among yourself and others (such as the allies you find in a few spirits or even in other witches; each connection serves to extend your awareness, extend the reach of your magick, and amplify the work you do because you're no longer operating within the self-imposed vacuum of presumed separation).

And so, the reminders of the inherent lack of separation, the need for wholeness, and the importance of connection become more greatly visible around you, making it easier to act from a place of wholeness. Those reminders can be found in:

- the way the spirit world (Otherworld) exists in the same space as the physical world, layered atop it

- the way that your spirit body is intimately connected to your physical body, a very real part of what you are, and that the only disconnection that can occur is in death

- the emphasis on community, viewing yourself not as individual against the world but as "one among many" and an integral piece in a web of connection, affecting others and directly impacting the quality of their life as much as they are affecting you, bound to others in obligation to do right by them so that all can experience greater potential for happiness and well-being in life

The Work of the Witch

The work of the witch, in large part, comes down to better understanding your place in the world within the context of everything that it has taught you and shown you to be true—recognizing that this craft provides you a unique set of skills that allows you to serve as a bridge and shine light upon the inherent lack of separation within the world for others. In this way, the witch is a mediary between the physical world and spirit world, operating with "a foot in both worlds" (as the saying goes), fostering a connection for those who aren't sure how to forge that connection on their own.

This work as a bridge can take many forms, such as more blatant actions like performing divination for a friend facing a crossroads in life or cleansing and warding the home of a family member recovering from prolonged illness. But it can also take far more subtle forms, such as pointing out to a neighbor the benefit of waiting to mow until after the spring ephemerals have bloomed so native pollinators have greater access to food or being present at just the right moment to convey a message to someone (be that message gleaned from intuition or a spirit—such as one of their ancestors or one of your familiars who is capable of seeing the situation better than you are). There are so many ways that your presence in the lives of others can help make more apparent the lack of separation that exists in the world, and so many ways to encourage a community-focused mindset in those closest to you.

But this work—this doing of witchcraft—is only possible when you act from a place founded on the wholeness of yourself and founded on the relationships you maintain—the community of which you are a part and that includes your local spirits just as much as your human family and friends. When you act from a place of acknowledgment of that interconnection and interwoven being, all magick you do will be stronger. You will not be working as yourself alone. That magick, because of your close relationships, becomes a community action. This holds true regardless of what the magick is—whether you're working to get money to cover the bills, entering trance and journeying, passing through a spirit-heavy location in the physical world, or warding your home. Your relationships with the spirits around you and the living humans closest to you seats you more fully into the web of being that exists across the layers of the world.

Awareness of that wholeness and connection comes with obligations. We've noted how to be in community with someone means to be bound in obligation to them. But there is obligation to yourself, too, especially in the form of personal responsibility. Knowledge that does not change how you behave is not knowledge that is fully appreciated. And so, knowledge of the connection you have to others requires you to hold yourself accountable for your actions as much as the knowledge of the layered reality of your being requires you to treat the layers of yourself—physical body and spirit body—with equal importance. It is hypocritical to change your behavior to account for the spirits with whom you share your home and the land but to not change your behavior so as to account for the well-being and care of your spirit body.

Rippling Outward

As witches, we exist in that space where the physical world and the spirit world intersect, and where the reality of a world alive with spirits butts harshly against a "civilized world" that refuses belief in such beings. So, this intersection—this awareness of the reality of many people (spirit and human) and of the lack of separation between the worlds crashing into the expectations and dominant attitudes of Western society—creates complications in our lives.

These complications largely stem from the incompatibility of animism with the dominant overculture. This incompatibility forces us to lean even harder into the personal responsibility that witchcraft demands of us. There are no easy answers when it comes to solving these complications and challenges. And, unfortunately, once you begin peeling back the layers, unpacking ideas you hold that don't support your developing animist worldview, the prevalence of these complications can feel overwhelming. Once you see the ways that a community-based worldview ripples outward, it is just as easy to see the ways that an individualist-based worldview ripples and influences everything.

For example, how do you rectify the harm caused by factory farmed meat when you're already struggling to afford food that isn't heavily processed? How do you treat the objects in your life with respect when your home is overflowing with stuff and you need to get rid of things for your own mental and physical health? How do you seek relationships with other living humans that are founded in right relationship when you've been burned so many times before? How do you uplift more marginalized members of your community when you're already overwhelmed with trying to attend to your own needs? How do you maintain relationships with family members you love whose opinions and views you find morally offensive and in opposition to all the changes you're trying to make to live more animistically?

There is inherent risk in making the choice to let animism change you, to let it change your witchcraft practice and let it change your life. There is risk of unsettling your life, of changing the dynamic of your closest relationships—of no longer fitting in or being able to pretend to fit in, of daring to live your life in a way that places you in opposition to a society that demands conformity. This isn't hyperbole: changing your worldview to one that contrasts sharply against the dominant worldview of the society in which you live has consequences.

There is the potential to feel alienated from others in your efforts to greater prioritize community and connection, and that alienation can come with those you might expect to be most understanding and supportive—such as other witches. For example, your efforts to more fully embrace animism may cause you to turn away from your current witchcraft practice, building a new practice: one that is spirit-led and prioritizes the information and techniques you learn from those spirits with whom you've forged close relationships. This can have you rejecting common practices such as the heavy reliance upon correspondences, or the appeal to authority that is behind the unearned trust placed in information simply because it's in a traditionally published book or posted by someone with a large social media following.

Just as it's not uncommon to find your relationships with friends and family becoming strained due to your worldview becoming more apparent in your actions, it's also not weird to find your relationships with the witches closest to you becoming strained, too. This can be for similar reasons as those we noted above in regard to the general witchcraft community, but one of the consequences of sinking yourself deeper into animism is becoming more aware of power dynamics and systems of hierarchy that are present within your interpersonal relationships—in addition to those playing out and present more broadly—and how there is too often a pattern in regards to the types of people being held down.

And while this is quite common (because witches do not exist in a vacuum and absolutely reflect and model the same issues that are found in the dominant overculture), it can be painful to discover that you are in a relationship with someone that lacks reciprocity and mutual support, or that requires you to hold parts of yourself back to maintain peace. You may even find some relationships quickly fall apart once you begin talking about your new experiences and how they're changing how you view things. It is, sadly, not unusual to find that in your efforts to decenter yourself in your spiritual practice and relationship with the world around you, others will respond by decentering and no longer making an effort to include you in their life.

You may also find the general pattern of your thought processes changing, with non-linear thinking becoming more natural for you. Adopting non-linear thinking (if it is not already your norm) is a typical consequence as it is complementary to animism due to how it emphasizes the relationships among ideas and the way those relationships are necessary for problem solving; it prioritizes the many and the many connections over one singular direct path and outcome. It allows for innovation, adaptation, and greater responsiveness to your environment, as it prioritizes the way that things fit into a space and affect—and are affected by—the space and others within that space. In this way, non-linear thinking is more holistic, taking into account the entire context and as many contributing factors as possible in order to, for example, develop a plan of action that adversely impacts as few people as possible.

Nonlinear thinking is also essential in spirit work as the spirits with whom we are interacting (especially in the Otherworld) have a very different culture and way of interacting with and perceiving the world and others. This is a really great example of another reason that learning to decenter yourself and living humans, in general, is such an important part of living your animism—spirits are not living humans and they do not hold our specific culturally influenced views and opinions. Even the spirit of a deceased human will not have the same views as a living human. To expect any type of spirit to behave in a way you assume is common to all living humans (which is already an erroneous assumption, different people are different and this applies to living humans, too) is to center yourself, to center your experiences, to disrespect that spirit, and to try to impose your way of being and worldview onto them. This will not yield the results wanted or needed when trying to interact with that spirit. And depending on the type of spirit and what you're trying to achieve, this could create larger problems for you that require additional action—like needing to purify yourself, cleanse your home, and ward yourself and home to put an end to some sudden parasitic behavior from a spirit now affecting your dreams and emotional health.

Ultimately, for as much beauty and wonder as becoming an animist can reveal to you in the world, changing your life in so many incredible ways, it isn't uncommon to question your decision to do so. The period of time between the potential loss of relationships and the building of new ones can make the prizing of community feel very lonely. It can also be very disconcerting to realize how unsupported your needs were in your closest relationships.

And it can feel quite overwhelming as you begin to see just how different—and hostile—the overculture is to animism and that you have a personal responsibility to do what you can to counter that influence, to awaken as many people as you can to a different way of being in the world. But animism doesn't ask us to solve the world's problems. In truth: we can't. Not alone. The hope that animism holds and the benefit it offers to us is rooted in community—with the Land and with each other. Any solution to any problem is likewise anchored in a land-based understanding of community. All that's asked of you is to do what you can to act with integrity and to take care of those closest to you—human and non-human.

While no individual can solve these problems, there is concrete power in building true community—power that ripples outward and makes our personal efforts to tug at that knot behind all these oppressive systems far more effective. And that is something we can do: we can put ourselves out there, be vulnerable, and strive to be in right relationship with each other, knowing that the impact of doing so reaches farther than we can imagine.

Exercises

Throughout this book, you've engaged in a variety of exercises to stretch your perspective and your witch skills, finding ways in which both can be different and more than what you may have previously thought was possible. Although not much time has passed, you've made significant progress in developing and growing competent with the basic skills of witchcraft—awareness, discipline, discernment, energy work, focus, strength of Will, and visualization. This effort will be noticeable in other areas of your practice and not just within the specific exercises you've been practicing, and the benefits of that effort will continue to reveal themselves to you. You may notice changes in your general psychic/spiritual sensitivity, as well as an increase in intensity of your spell work. You may also notice your divinatory readings becoming more accurate, with messages and connections coming far more easily than before.

For our final lesson, you will be completing an in-depth journal prompt, taking your efforts to develop a relationship with the Land further, and continuing to focus on practicing previous exercises in order to strengthen your skills. Some suggestions are included to help you continue the work you've been doing to sink yourself deeper into the Land and animism. These are starting points for exploration and can be modified and expanded upon. Use them as a springboard to have further experiences and discoveries.

Exercise 1: Walking the Talk—Journal Prompt

For this journal prompt, you will be thinking critically about your witchcraft practice and your life in regard to your deepening animist worldview. Remember that to think critically about something doesn't mean to only look for or point out things that could be considered negative or faulty—and the point of this exercise is absolutely not focused solely on looking for or finding problems. Rather, critical thinking involves a full consideration of something. This isn't just looking at the pros and cons, the "good" and the "bad," the progress and the challenges yet to be faced. It's also considering the way something fits into the big picture, the connections that spread outward, the impact that one part has on another part as well as the entire whole. It's looking at something in regard to how it relates to everything around it and potentially finding ways that it holds a relationship to things outside of that immediate proximity.

Because of this, the following questions are truly only starting points. There are so many directions in which you could head based on any of these questions; it is highly advised to let your thoughts wander and to turn this into a discernment exercise, allowing yourself to engage in deep contemplation for the realizations and insights that could be uncovered as a result.

As always, there is no right or wrong way to approach this activity. You can freewrite, spilling words across the page until every thought has run its course. You could write each question down and then respond in lists, taking each list point as far as you feel comfortable or so moved to explore. You could create a mind map in order to better see the ways that your responses to some of these questions relate to each other, perhaps making it easier to see how some challenges have already solved themselves or the ways in which you've been making greater progress than was readily apparent to you due to how consistent you've been with that progress.

Try to give yourself at least thirty minutes to write, however, you may find your thoughts consuming you for longer than that. You can always complete this exercise in small chunks of time or even revisit these questions again in the future.

Remember, there are no right or wrong answers to any of these questions. The purpose is to better help you identify your place in the web of community around you and the impact that you have on that web.

Consider your witchcraft practice: are there any practices in which you've been engaging that don't make sense in an animist context? If so, is it a matter of incompatibility where these practices do not demonstrate your values? Do these practices serve an important purpose or does the need they were intended to fulfill no longer exist for you? If that need still exists but this practice doesn't align with your animist values, what can you do instead to fulfill that need while still holding true to your values?

Are there additional changes that could be made within your witchcraft to bring your practice into better alignment with your deeper understanding of animism? This could be something like devoting one day out of every lunar cycle to spending time with the land spirits around your home, talking with them, and leaving formal offerings to help maintain your relationship with them, or maybe as thanks for their help in protecting you and your home from transient spirits who might cause trouble, anything they've taught you, or for any assistance that they've offered you with your witchcraft. Or it might be reconsidering the materials you use in your practice. Now that you have a burgeoning relationship with your local land spirits, grow—or acquire from your local area, with permission—your own herbs, rather than using ones from unknown sources.

What about outside of your witchcraft practice? What changes are you beginning to see take hold in your behavior and your interactions with others that are a direct result of your expanding perspective? Are there aspects of the way you live your life that stand in strong contrast to your deepening values? Have any of your relationships with friends or family members revealed themselves

as needing attention as they demonstrate a lack of reciprocity—
either towards you or from you?

What about your relationships with people you don't really
know? Has your deeper exploration of animism revealed ways that
you have already been striving to be in right relationship with people in your broader community that you don't personally know?
Have you discovered opportunities to make changes in your attitude and behavior toward others that more accurately reflect the
importance of being in community with them?

Exercise 2: Introducing Yourself

As part of your continued efforts (began in Lesson 3: A World
Alive with Spirits and continued in Lesson 6: The Layered World)
to strengthen your relationship with the Land by increasing your
familiarity with a specific location, you will be revisiting the location you've chosen to build upon your efforts in a way that may
yield surprising results. On this visit, you will be deliberately introducing yourself to and attempting to have a conversation with at
least three land spirits.

Pause at the border of this location and reach out to the guardian spirit in a similar way as you did on your last visit (close your
eyes, center, gently extend your awareness outward toward the border, acknowledge the existence of the guardian spirit—even if you
don't feel them or have indication of their presence). As this is your
second attempt to interact with them, it is more likely for you to
receive some sort of indication of their presence this time if you
didn't previously. Given the type of spirit they are and that you have

previously visited this location in a respectful manner, you are likely to be met with quiet alertness and maybe even curiosity.

If you do have clear indication of their presence and them acknowledging you, hold yourself in that moment, keeping your awareness open and gently extended toward them. Do not push your energy onto them, just hold yourself open so that you can feel what can be felt and experience what can be experienced. You may find it helps to open your eyes or to keep them closed.

Similar to the Defining your Borders exercise of Lesson 5: The Layered Witch, where you gently ran your awareness along the borders of your seat of consciousness, your physical body, and your spirit body, gently run your awareness along the edges of the guardian spirit. Be sure to stay alert for any indication that your actions are undesired and to withdraw immediately if you receive such. As you do so, you may get mental imagery of what they look like, a better idea of their personality and what their expectations are for you, or even an impression of their range. They may even communicate with you, letting you know of areas you should avoid or encouraging you to visit specific locations. If anything is asked of you—and it's something you can accomplish, like being shown a specific area that has been subjected to dumping and clearly being asked to clean it up—make an attempt to do so on this visit.

When the sensations and impressions you received grow quiet, convey your intentions for the visit (to enter the location, wander around, and introduce yourself to some of the spirits that call this location home) and pause to allow time for a response to be given. You very likely will not receive a firm confirmation that you can proceed. It's more common to only receive a firm no, if any sort of response.

Alive with Spirits

At this point, you probably have a good idea of where to go from here and which spirit to approach. You may have had a good interaction with a spirit during your last visit; this would be a good conversation to continue. Generally, it is advisable to stick to spirits that are bound to some sort of object, such as a plant, tree, stone, river, or hill. Some excellent choices would be the spirits of plants or trees that have been focal points in your research. The wandery types of spirits who can be found out on the land yet who are not bound to any physical object—these tend to be less predictable in their responses. They also generally tend to be more difficult to seek and actually find (that is, you tend to happen upon them), with many types being the exact types of spirits you don't want to encounter.

Approach these spirits in a similar manner as you followed in Exercise 1: Seeking Interaction of the previous lesson. Once you have amiable contact, initiate a conversation with that spirit. What might you talk about? If they are a spirit of one of the plants or trees that you've been researching, you could talk to them about your research, mentioning how you've read that they might be helpful for a particular magickal use or that they have a particular effect on the human body. You could talk to them about the area in which they're growing, expressing your fondness for the location. You could talk about your efforts to be more connected to the land and to develop strong relationships with its spirits.

Pay attention to the responses you receive—they may surprise you. Some spirits may communicate with you in words that you hear as clearly as you read these words, or the words may sort of appear in your thoughts. You may have impressions of colors or emotions. You may feel pressure at your forehead or the back of your head when you ask questions, with that pressure only appearing as a "yes" response. You may be shown imagery, you may feel your attention guided elsewhere and a compulsion to head in that direction. There are so many ways that a spirit may choose (or be able to) communicate with you. Hold yourself open and try to withhold any expectations.

When the conversation begins to wane or you feel yourself being encouraged to move on, thank that spirit for spending time with you and answering your questions. Slowly withdraw and wander about the location for a little bit before approaching another spirit.

Try to communicate with at least three different spirits, in order to potentially have a broader range of experiences. Be sure to thank the guardian spirit of that location when you leave for helping to ensure your safety.

Record your experiences in your notes, making sure to describe any physical sensations you had as well as the type of spirit with whom you were interacting.

Ongoing Exercises

- Continue to practice your energy exercises. Compare your results now to the results you first had. How have they become easier to do? Are you experiencing different sensations when doing them now? Don't skip over exercises that were easy to do the first time, you may find you have different results now. Regardless, repetition will always make your skills stronger.

- Consider the list of obstacles that you identified in Lesson 2: Witchcraft Comes from the Land. You've done so much work to help yourself further adopt an animist worldview since then; have any of these obstacles changed? We've noted how worldview affects the things that you think about, as well as the way that any topic is framed and approached. Are there any obstacles that have become irrelevant, not applying to your views now? Have new things come up that are serving as obstacles for you right now?

Continuing Practice

Changing your worldview is not something that can be accomplished quickly. Although you have done so much and had so many experiences to help show you firsthand how much more the world is, how much more you are, the time it takes to read one book is nowhere near long enough to truly adopt a new worldview—a new way of seeing and being in the world.

The work continues from here. To help you do that work, here are a few suggestions for long-term activities that can help you to further root yourself into your local land, helping you to be viewed as one who truly belongs there by your local land spirits, as well as helping you to add new depth to your witchcraft practice. Feel free to use these as the basis for deeper exploration and to add to this list; these are only a few potential starting points.

- Chart the lunar cycle. The natural world is ruled by cycles, and that very much includes yourself. It isn't uncommon to find that, in working to deepen your connection to the

Land, the cycles playing out upon your local landscape begin to affect you more heavily. Document the way that the eight phases of the lunar cycle (dark moon, waxing crescent, first quarter moon, waxing gibbous, full moon, waning gibbous, third quarter moon, waning crescent) affect you. What is your general mood during each phase? How are you sleeping? Are you dreaming more or less? How is your focus? How does your physical body feel? Do you have pain or tension during certain phases? Is your intuition stronger at certain times? Are certain magickal activities, like trance or energy exercises using personal energy, easier or more difficult to accomplish during certain phases? Do you find spirit communication easier or more challenging?

• Chart the lunar cycle but note the ways the Land responds. Do the plants outside your home appear fuller or droopy during certain phases? Does it rain more often during a particular phase? Do you catch sight of wandering spirits at certain phases? Are the spirits in your home more or less communicative? What about the land spirits with whom you most frequently interact? Is plant material you gather (with permission) more or less potent when gathered during certain lunar phases versus others?

• Pay attention to the seasons and note the way that your local land responds to the solar cycle. What defines each season? Are there more seasons where you live than the standard four? Different seasons? What dominant and subtle changes are taking place on the land? What changes in the land indicate the start of each season? What changes in behavior do you notice among the various land spirits you regularly encounter? Are there patterns that play out in particular seasons that aren't evident in others?

· Consider ways that you can implement these cycles into your witchcraft practice. For example, you might charge water with the light of the sun or moon, taking into account the effects of the local expression of the seasons, and use that water throughout your practice (for example, to anoint candles in spell work, to anoint the vessels of familiars, as the base for making dyes and inks, as the base for infusions, or to scry by).

· Seek the wisdom of the Land. Everything you need to be a witch—including the knowledge of witchcraft—can be gotten directly from the Land. The next time you find yourself facing a challenging situation in your practice and need some guidance, turn to the Land for advice on what to do rather than checking out books and websites. Has a strained relationship with a family member suddenly gotten worse? Ask the land spirits with whom you've been growing close how you might remedy this situation, perhaps to keep yourself safe and also help that family member to be more cognizant of their actions. Have you encountered a recurring problem in your life and nothing you do seems to help you get unstuck? Talk to your house spirits and get their perspective. They spend more time with you than anyone else, and they know what's going on in the house more than anyone else—including if there is a new spirit causing trouble, a gap in your warding, an unintentional magickal attack lodged at you from a jealous friend, or something you're doing that is causing or contributing to the stagnation. They may be able to identify what's wrong as well as provide you an effective means of handling the situation.

· Work with the land for its benefit. As part of your efforts to identify local plants and trees, you likely discovered a few plants that are invasives—plants that originated somewhere else, evolving in a different environment with different pollinators, and whose presence in the local landscape is destructive due to how that plant outcompetes native plants, does not provide food for native pollinators, and has not evolved with local wildlife so as to be used as a food source and have its growth kept in check. Expand upon your research to see how you can remove these invasive plants from your local landscape (allowing native plants to take their place) and put them to use. Can they be eaten? If so, what are some realistic ways that you could add them to your meals (for example, in a salad, as pesto; do they need to be cooked first)? If not, or if eating invasives isn't practical or healthy for you, what are other ways that you can put them to use? Can you compost them? Can you make cording from them that you could use in your witchcraft practice, perhaps for knot magick or making jewelry? What do your conversations with these invasive plants reveal? Are there magickal uses to which they could be put to use, perhaps as a spell ingredient or perhaps replacing an herb you once used heavily but are removing from your practice for ethical reasons (like poached white sage or frankincense)?

Alive with Spirits

- Continue to explore the place you've been visiting (as part of these exercises) in the Otherworld. Have you discovered more differences—or similarities—between the way you experience this place in the physical versus the spirit world? You previously went visiting and made a point of noticing any spots that might be portals to the Otherworld: have you confirmed this yet? Have you practiced entering trance near these portals to see what might happen? Have you attempted to travel through them, either to journey via your spirit body or to see if you can get a handle on world walking? In the Otherworld, have you found any trails heading away from this familiar place? Have you figured out where any of them lead yet (and if not, are you ready to take some precautions to keep yourself safe and make that trip)?

Final Note

In that way that witchcraft likes to embrace contradiction, it is a fluid practice, resisting our attempts to nail it firm. Yet in its practice, through its enaction and through living life as a witch and animist, we find that witchcraft serves to root us down, to anchor us within local space so that we better belong and more healthfully operate—on a physical and spiritual level—within that distinct location.

Actually being present in the world, recognizing that the world is filled with people—human people, spirit people, plant people, stone people, river people, cloud people—demands that we take accountability for ourselves and for our lifestyles. That requires us to be uncomfortable, to be sad, to be angry, to feel hopeless, to change, and to promise to do and be better. That's the real power of witchcraft, that it shows us who we are and demands we do better, that it shows us how the world really is.

Although you've reached the end of this book, the process of learning to live as an animist continues. Witchcraft is a toolkit for seeing our world more fully for what it is and for effectively navigating the realities of that multilayered reality. Embrace its practice and continue the work you've begun. Your efforts will continue to reveal new layers to the world around you and you will continue to have experiences that show you just how much more there is to the world—and to yourself.

Glossary

altered state. See trance

ancestors. Spirits of deceased humans to whom one is bound due to the peculiarities of existing as a creature made of both flesh and spirit; ancestors can refer to spirits who would commonly be considered family (having a connection with us through genetics, marriage, or love) but the term can also refer to those people who came before us who contributed greatly to our spiritual development, such as leaders in religious traditions to which we belong, teachers, and even authors (these types of ancestors are commonly referred to as mighty dead while familial ancestors are then referred to as beloved dead).

animism. The oldest known worldview among human kind, it is founded on the idea of wholeness and a lack of separation among all beings, as well as between the physical world and the spirit world. It prioritizes community over the individual, understanding that the actions of the individual affect the community and the health and well-being of the community affects the health and well-being of the individual. As it is a worldview, the details will present differently within different religions and cultures (such as in differences regarding qualifications for personhood) while consistently emphasizing community and that personhood extends to more than just humans (such as also extending to spirits, natural features of the landscape, plants, animals, and spirits). As a term, animism was coined by Sir Edward Burnett Tylor in Primitive Culture (1871), however his usage was derogatory and helped further encourage an extractive approach to the study of Indigenous people and non-Christian religions.

awareness. One of the foundational skills of witchcraft, it is the skill of paying attention without expectations or judgment; a passive state of receptivity in which you experience what is there to be experienced, being open to the subtlety of spiritual forces (energy) within and without you.

blasting rod. A ritual tool crafted from wood, about an arm's length, and used for the purposeful sending out of energy typically for baleful or more aggressive reasons. They are also used in the creation of altered time and space, such as with the throwing of a compass. Often, a walking stick will be rendered a blasting rod.

breath work. The practice of using breath as a means of manipulating energy and inducing an altered state of consciousness.

centering. A spiritual technique that reorients one within themselves, bringing balance between one's physical body and spirit body, as well as reorienting one within the physical world and spirit world; it is useful as a precursor to magickal action—such as spirit communication, divination, energy exercises, spellcraft, or other ritual, compare with grounding.

channel. An energetic space that runs the length of your spine and along which energy flows; energy can be deliberately pulled into and moved along this space as a means of potent energy exercise as well as a means of accessing energy from outside oneself and using that energy to achieve various magickal results.

dead zone. A physical location that has experienced trauma in such a way that resulted in the removal of the spirits who called that location home, such as a recently clear cut forest or a house that was heavily remodeled; dead zones typically heal on their own but that healing can be facilitated.

discipline. One of the foundational skills of witchcraft, it is the skill of being able to follow through, to identify a problem and then do the work necessary to solve it.

discernment. Within witchcraft, it is one of the seven foundational skills and a practice; as a skill, it is your ability to tell this from that; the skill of being able to accurately interpret and identify spiritual forces (including energy, spirit presence, and spirit communication) as distinct from other spiritual forces as well as from non-spiritual sources. As a practice, it is the use of awareness and focus skills as part of active contemplation for the purpose of gaining insight into a matter.

divination. Any variety of methods of gathering information, through the use of spiritual skills to analyze and interpret spiritual forces, that are reliant upon the use of physical objects; divination is a way for us to take a snapshot of the energy currents surrounding a person or situation; there exist hundreds of divination modalities, some popular methods include: Tarot, runes, Ogham, cartomancy, and throwing the bones.

dualism. A worldview that frequently accompanies monotheism and is founded on separation between the physical and the spiritual, including a separation between living humans and the one singular deity, as well as between living humans and the dead.

embodied practice. The conjoined use of physical body and spirit body, it is putting into practice the recognition of the physical body as a place where spiritual experiences occur and that it is not possible to have a spiritual experience without use of the physical body; witchcraft, as a spiritual practice, is an embodied craft as it cannot be practiced without connection to and use of the physical—be that our physical bodies or the physical world.

energy. A colloquial term referring to subtle spiritual forces present within all physical things as well as existing separate (and distinct) from physical things; it is not able to be measured or experienced except through the use of spiritual skills and thus cannot currently be proven; it is not the same energy spoken of in any branch of science and no one knows, conclusively, what it is—just that something is there that we can affect and be affected by; the manipulation of energy is the foundation of magickal practice.

energy work. The art and practice of manipulating energy, energy can generally be manipulated in three ways: pushed, pulled, or held; energy work is the foundation of magickal practice and one of the foundational skills of witchcraft.

familiar. A spirit with whom a witch has an intimate and deeply personal relationship that is predicated on the ritual binding of that spirit to the witch; as a familiar is a spirit, it is able to perform numerous magickal tasks for the witch, including boosting spellcraft, acquiring information, protection, and serving as a guide while journeying.

focus. One of the foundational skills of witchcraft, it is the skill of paying attention but with concentration applied to a purpose; where awareness is passive and objective, focus is active and specific.

folk magic. A body of information relative to the common people of a specific region that relates to spiritual beliefs, superstitions, customs, and the position that people hold within the local land, as well as those practices utilized to better help the individual and their community navigate that position, be in right relationship with the land and its spirits, and otherwise better their position in life.

grounding. A spiritual technique that creates a complete energetic circuit between oneself, the Earth, and the cosmos, thereby balancing the flow of energy within you and reorienting you within the world; it is frequently performed as an energy exercise, as well as in conjunction with centering prior to magickal action, compare with centering.

inscendence. A process of sinking back into the source, of seeking the core of the world and becoming tangled up with the heart of it, with life and living; a descriptive process that is the goal of witchcraft as a spiritual practice: where other spiritual practices may seek transcendence (to rise above and beyond the physical world and the physicality of the individual) witchcraft seeks inscendence, to sink deeper into the land and the physical; as a term, it was coined by Thomas Berry.

journeying. A spiritual technique in which one travels, via the use of their spirit body, to the Otherworld (spirit world); also known as walking between the worlds, traveling to the spirit world, spirit flight, and astral travel.

Land, the. With purposeful capitalization, "the Land" refers to the intersection of the physical world with the spirits that inhabit it, particularly those spirits whom would be termed land spirits; as a term, its use is dependent upon the recognition of the layering of the physical world and the spirit world; the source of witchcraft.

land spirits. A broad term that includes a number of greatly varying spirits who share a connection to the physical world. This connection can be due to that spirit being bound to a natural physical object (such as a stone, river, or plant), a natural process (such as the wind or an ocean current), a location (such as the guardian spirit of a forest), or because that spirit primarily exists within the physical world (such as trolls).

landscape. The intersection of the physical land with the culture upon it, recognizing the unfolding stories taking place upon the land; landscape is a fluid and dynamic place, one that is endlessly changing and becoming.

liminality. A state of existing in between one thing and another; liminal locations can be powerful places in witchcraft, as there exists inherent unknown potential that the witch can make use of, such as using a naturally occurring archway created by two trees as a doorway to the Otherworld or using a fence line as a means of slipping into trance and gathering information from a location near to another fence line.

magick. The action of utilizing spiritual forces to create change; there are many different systems and approaches to magick, each with their own foci and goals, witchcraft is but one example of a system of magick.

monotheism. A worldview that proposes one singular deity who exists within and separate from the physical world; it frequently is accompanied by dualism.

Otherworld. Also referred to as the spirit world, this is another plane of reality that is layered atop the physical world and in which all beings are comprised of energy; the name Otherworld emphasizes the quality of "other" about the spirit world, how it is like the physical world yet so very different.

Paganism. A contemporary new religious movement which adopted the name Paganism in the 1960's and has traditionally focused on inspired revivalism of pre-Christian European and Mediterranean religions; it is comprised of numerous religions, traditions, and spiritual practices which are largely (but not always) polytheistic and animistic.

panentheism. A worldview similar to pantheism yet differing in that "the divine" or "god" is viewed as being imminent (within all physicality) and transcendent (existing separate from all physicality).

pantheism. A worldview founded on the belief that "the divine" or "god" exists in all things and that physicality is the manifestation of them. Rather than unique and individual spirits within all things, there is part of a greater divine whole that is present in all things; that divine essence does not exist outside of its presence in physical matter nor in an individual manner, contrast with panentheism.

parasitic spirits. Types of spirits that naturally feed off of other beings to sustain themselves, much the same way that parasitic creatures exist in the physical world; an example are the common yet easily removed energy leaches that appear like lampreys attached to the spirit body.

place. A site that is defined by relationships: the experiences had there, the meaning attached to it, and the emotional connection to that location.

polytheism. A worldview founded on the existence of many, living, complex, individual, and autonomous deities who exist within and without the physical world and whose presence and actions maintain order in the cosmos; although not the same as animism, the two are compatible and frequently coexist; an ancient yet still widespread and common religious worldview, contrast with monotheism.

portal. Any sort of space that can be used as a doorway to the Otherworld; they can be purposely created (such as by collecting crossroads dirt and creating a crossroads inside your home), they can be created out of a preexisting structure (such as a doorway or fence line), or they can be naturally occurring (such as the border of a forest and meadow, or any place where land meets sky meets water).

right relationship. The actions you take that are congruent with the awareness of the relationship that exists between you and another being, the awareness of inarguable autonomy of each of you and the awareness of your mutual obligations to each other as a result; acting in such a way so as to minimize negative impact upon the beings closest to you and in such a way so as to encourage and work toward mutual benefit for all, as much as is possible.

ritual. Any series of steps that can be repeated in order to consistently achieve similar results; examples of ritual (within the context of witchcraft) can include spells, the making of offerings to Gods and other spirits, or even preparatory actions performed prior to divination.

shielding. A spiritual technique in which you create an energetic barrier around yourself for the purpose of more effectively keeping personal energy contained and to prevent the unwanted influence of outside sources of energy (this could include preventing energetic access to you as a form of protection from other living humans or spirits); shielding can also be used as part of "invisibility magick" to make yourself less noticeable when passing through a location.

sign. Any sort of occurrence to which meaning that does not exist inherently within that context can be assigned to that occurrence; signs can be used as a form of communication by some spirits, however, most signs that we encounter will not be spirit communication; signs generally hold meaning and relevance only to the person experiencing them in that moment; signs are distinguished not by the potential for assigning meaning to them nor to what that meaning is but by the energetic presence that fills that moment, creating a quality of alterity (otherness) and resulting in various spiritual sensations by the person experiencing that sign.

spells. A concentrated and deliberate act of magick for the purpose of creating specific change. It utilizes spiritual forces to create measurable changes in the energy within or without a situation or person.

spirit. A spectrum of beings that exist primarily in energetic form; some of these beings once possessed physical form, some currently possess or are bound to physical form, some have never possessed physical form and never will, some exist bound to natural objects, some exist within man-made objects; a diverse range of people who exist primarily in energetic form.

spirit work. The art and practice of interacting and communicating with spirit people, it encompasses the relationships you have with spirits as well as the skills necessary for you to build and maintain those relationships

spirit world. See Otherworld.

stang. A ritual tool used to aid in journeying to the Otherworld, to alter space and time as part of magickal working, for magickal defense, and as a vehicle through which spirits may be called. Made of wood, they may be forked on one end or, alternately, be topped with a horned or antlered skull. Sometimes a candle will be nailed between the tines or affixed to the skull between the horns/antlers.

synchronicity. Repeated occurrences that happen in relatively close succession of each other yet have no apparent connection to each other. It is often stated that something is not synchronicity until it happens three times, however, it is the energetic presence in that moment and defining that occurrence that makes something be a sync and not the power of any numerical value, synchronicity can occur because we find ourselves repeatedly encountering intersecting currents of energy and not as any sort of message for us personally, compare with signs.

trance. The ways in which a witch makes use of the fluidity of consciousness to magickal ends; an altered state of consciousness that occurs as part of the way humans naturally function when performing magickal actions such as divination, spells, spirit communication, healing work, or journeying to the Otherworld.

visualization. One of the foundational skills of witchcraft, it is the skill of simulating spiritual sensations by recreating the accompanying physical sensations through your mind thus creating a bridge between the physical body and spirit body that allows for more accurate use of the spirit body as part of magickal action.

witchcraft. A contemporary system of magick that takes great inspiration from various European folk magic practices of the last few hundred years and is defined by its inclusion of five traits: animism (as a worldview), divination (as a means of gathering information), the Land (as its originating source of wisdom and materials), ritual (as a method of and structure for action), and spirit work (the embodied nature of witchcraft as expressed through the actions of the witch); due to the historical and ongoing efforts of Christianity to acquire and maintain hegemonic control over various peoples, the religiomagical practices of any given culture have typically been labeled "witchcraft," however, what we commonly term witchcraft is a specific contemporary spiritual practice, arising in the 20th century;

folklore and folk magic practices of any culture do not, in themselves, constitute witchcraft; compare with folk magic.

Will. With deliberate capitalization, Will is the powering factor behind magickal action that is inherent to the individual and must be developed. The strength of one's Will is impacted by their justified confidence in their skills and themselves, as well as one's sense of self. Will is the knowledge that if we take hold of energy, shape it, and hurtle it at a target, we will get the results we want because we are applying skills through desire and so it becomes the means of that taking hold, shaping, and hurtling.

world walking. A spiritual technique for simultaneously experiencing the physical world and the spirit world; a technique in which you remain grounded and moving within the physical world while focused on and interacting with the spirit world as layered over top the physical world.

worldview. The fundamental perception of the world that influences how one thinks about the world and how one moves through the world; it affects how you see yourself, how you see others, how you treat yourself, how you treat others, and how you justify those thoughts and actions; the why behind your actions.

About the Author

Althaea Sebastiani is a full-time spiritworker and religious educator whose work focuses on helping people navigate the realities of deep spiritual practice. Her work primarily takes the forms of spiritual counseling and education framed within the contexts of animism and witchcraft. She contends that witchcraft is a tool that enables us to see—and interact with—the world more honestly. She is the author of several books including *By Rust of Nail and Prick of Thorn*. Find her @LadyAlthaea or at *ladyalthaea.com*.